DIRECT MARKETING TECHNIQUES

Building Your Business Using Direct Mail and Direct Response Advertising

Lois K. Geller

A FIFTY-MINUTE™ SERIES BOOK

DIRECT MARKETING TECHNIQUES

Building Your Business Using Direct Mail and Direct Response Advertising

Lois K. Geller

CREDITS
Senior Editor: **Debbie Woodbury**
Assistant Editor: **Genevieve Del Rosario**
Production Manager: **Denise Powers**
Typesetting: **ExecuStaff**
Cover Design: **Nicole Phillips**

For more information contact:

> Course Technology
> 25 Thomson Place
> Boston, MA 02210

Or find us on the Web at **www.courseilt.com**

For permission to use material from this text or product, submit a request online at www.thomsonrights.com.

Trademarks
Crisp Learning is a trademark of Course Technology. Some of the product names and company names used in this book have been used for identification purposes only, and may be trademarks or registered trademarks of their respective manufacturers and sellers.

Disclaimer
Course Technology reserves the right to revise this publication and make changes from time to time in its content without notice.

ISBN 1-56052-474-X
Library of Congress Catalog Card Number 98-70114
Printed in Canada by Webcom Limited

2 3 4 5 PM 06 05 04

LEARNING OBJECTIVES FOR:

DIRECT MARKETING TECHNIQUES

The objectives for *Direct Marketing Techniques* are listed below. They have been developed to guide you, the reader, to the core issues covered in this book.

Objectives

- ❑ 1) **To show ways to build your business with direct marketing.**

- ❑ 2) **To explain a direct marketing campaign.**

- ❑ 3) **To show how to use direct response advertising.**

Assessing Your Progress

In addition to the learning objectives above, Course Technology has developed a Crisp Series **assessment** that covers the fundamental information presented in this book. A 25-item, multiple-choice and true/false questionnaire allows the reader to evaluate his or her comprehension of the subject matter. To buy the assessment and answer key, go to www.courseilt.com and search on the book title or via the assessment format, or call 1-800-442-7477.

Assessments should not be used in any employee selection process.

ABOUT THE AUTHOR

Lois Geller is president of Mason & Geller, an advertising and public relations firm. Her clients have included such businesses as Time Inc., PolyGram Music and Crayola. Ms. Geller has been a Dale Carnegie instructor, a guest lecturer for several marketing groups and guest and keynote speaker for the Direct Marketing Association Conventions, and many others. She is an adjunct professor at New York University where she teaches the lead course in Direct Marketing. In May of 1997, Lois was awarded the New York University Award for Teaching Excellence.

Ms. Geller has authored and edited a number of books, including the 24-volume set of the New International Encyclopedia of Art and the New International Encyclopedia of Gardening. Her book, *Response!—The Complete Guide to Profitable Direct Marketing*, has been published in eight countries and serialized in many American marketing and advertising magazines.

ABOUT THE SERIES

With over 200 titles in print, the acclaimed Crisp 50-Minute™ series presents self-paced learning at its easiest and best. These comprehensive self-study books for business or personal use are filled with exercises, activities, assessments, and case studies that capture your interest and increase your understanding.

Other Crisp products, based on the 50-Minute books, are available in a variety of learning style formats for both individual and group study, including audio, video, CD-ROM, and computer-based training.

ACKNOWLEDGMENTS

Special acknowledgments and thanks go to Sharyn Kolberg, who helped me get this book written and out the door. She encouraged me to make the time to write it. She is wonderful and I am so grateful to her.

Special appreciation also goes to my parents, who believe in me and support everything I do. To Michael McCormick, who runs the workload at the agency; James (Pepper) Huff, a great person at getting things done; and Guy DeSemini, Patricia Sheridan, Charlie Mason, and Judy Smith.

Thanks also to my friends who stay my friends when I'm in isolation, writing. Those precious friends are Andrea Nierenberg; George McGreal; Norman Amiel; Judy and Mitch Milstein; Tom Amoriello; Murray Miller; and everyone else—you know who you are.

DEDICATION

When my son, Paul, was growing up, I always had a lot of ideas about how we could earn money using direct marketing. There had to be money for all the things a young man needs—orthodontia, band trips, special hobbies.

For a while, we had our own mail order jewelry business; there were freelance assignments in which we offered Guernsey stamps through the mail, an encyclopedia in one volume, and even Dolly Parton dolls.

Each program was an adventure because Paul helped me with the copy, figuring out response rates, working on strategy. He was great—he had a positive attitude and always encouraged me to go for it!

So I dedicate this book to my son, Paul, and his wonderful wife, Joan, who now encourages him to go for it . . . whatever his dream may be.

I wish the same for you, as a reader of this book. Read it, try it, and make your dreams happen.

DEAR READER:

Everywhere I go, people tell me they want to get into direct marketing.

- Some people (like the dry cleaner in my neighborhood) already have an established business and want to use direct marketing to expand their customer base.

- Other people (like my dentist, who has invented a golf hat through which you can listen to audio tapes to improve your golf swing) want to use direct marketing to supplement their current income.

- And still others (like the woman in Pennsylvania who has designed some really innovative dollhouses) want to make their living selling their product or service directly to consumers via direct marketing.

The Direct Marketing Miracle
Can Happen for You!

I've learned, after more than 25 years in this business, that anyone can make the direct marketing miracle happen. As with anything else you need to learn how to do, there are certain rules to follow, and much that is learned through trial and testing. You continue the programs that work and discard the ones that don't. It's as easy as that.

Direct marketing is a science with measurable results. When you learn how it works, you can estimate the costs of your campaign, determine your likely response, and figure out how much profit you can expect to make. Direct marketing encompasses direct mail, direct response print advertising, direct response television and radio advertising, telemarketing, and the Internet. This book is designed for those of you who are making your first foray into direct marketing; therefore, it concentrates on direct mail and direct response print advertising.

Direct Marketing—a $95 Billion Business

Businesses of all sizes are using direct marketing these days, from Fortune 500 companies with huge budgets to small entrepreneurs with home-based offices. Thousands of people have started small direct marketing businesses in their homes or garages. That's the way Lillian Vernon started her mega-catalog business.

Most successful direct marketers grow their businesses little by little, conservatively, with a small outlay of money. So whether you're coming to this book with a budget of a few thousand dollars or a lot more, you can get started immediately making your direct marketing dreams a reality.

The important thing is not to expect to make millions right off the bat. The idea is to build on each success, one by one. Get customers, keep the customers you have, then get more customers, and keep building a loyal customer base. Once you do, you'll have an ongoing business.

The people who succeed in this business are people who don't easily get disappointed. They know that if a direct mail campaign or direct response ad doesn't pull in as many orders as they want, they stick with it, testing new ideas and changing one aspect at a time until they come upon the right solution. They're tenacious, and they make it happen.

I Know, Because It Happened to Me

I started out with a small mail order business and built it over time. Now I have my own direct marketing agency and I help a lot of other people do the same thing. So I know it can happen, and it can happen for you.

The only way to begin is to turn the page, put together your plan, and stick with it. Just go through the chapters step-by-step, and when you're done go back and review them again. The more experience you get, the more comfortable you will become, and the more confidence you will have in offering your product or service through the mail.

Lots of good luck—and get started today!

Lois Geller

CONTENTS

Direct Marketing Techniques

CONTENTS (continued)

P A R T

I

How To Use Direct Marketing To Build Your Business

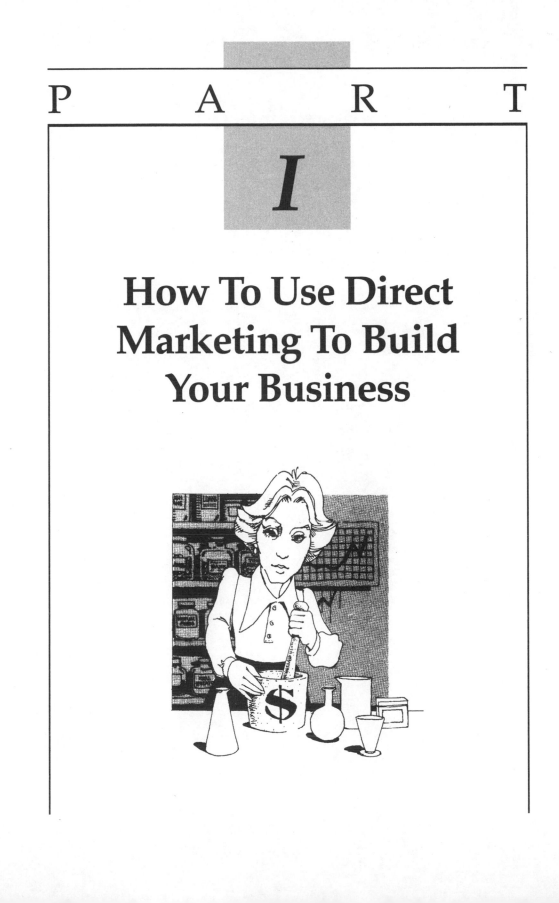

WHAT IS DIRECT MARKETING?

▶ Direct marketing is a measurable, tested marketing method whereby products or services are offered to a targeted audience and a direct response is solicited.

▶ Direct marketing is the most effective method of targeting a large number of people who, because they meet a certain set of criteria, are likely to buy your product.

▶ Direct marketing is a process of introducing yourself, your service, or your product, and forming a continuing relationship with a specially chosen group of potential customers.

▶ Direct marketing encompasses:

- *Direct mailers*—anything you mail out to people in which you're asking them to order something from you.

- *Direct response print advertising*—any ad that includes a toll-free order number, a coupon, or an order form for response.

- *Direct response television*—any ad that includes a toll-free number or address to mail in orders. That includes infomercials.

- *Direct response radio*—any ad that includes a toll-free number or address to mail in orders.

- *The Internet*—any Web site in which people are asked to place an order (or that gives a toll-free number to call to place an order).

- *Telemarketing*—any phone call in which people are asked to make a purchase.

WHY DIRECT MARKETING?

Not so long ago, we all had one-on-one relationships with the people who sold us products or services. We knew the owner of the grocery store on the corner; the barber or hairdresser knew our entire family history (the good, the bad, and the ugly); we lived next door to the one lawyer in town; and milk was delivered by the same person direct to our doorstep day after day.

Now every mall looks the same. Giant chain stores have forced Mom and Pop to retire long ago, and we buy many of our wordly goods without ever leaving the house. Most of us enjoy this new convenience but miss the human connection we used to have with merchants. That connection can be achieved through direct marketing, or what I prefer to call *relationship marketing*.

So what is this thing called direct marketing? There are many ways in which you can let people know about your business: advertising, promotion, and public relations. Any one of these can probably help build your business. Direct marketing is different because it is the only one that is accountable. Every time we do a direct mail campaign or run a direct response ad, we know within days (sometimes within hours) what kind of response we've gotten from that particular program. Direct marketing provides immediate results.

Once we get our first customers, we continue our relationship with them. We send them catalogs; we offer them more products; we call them on the phone; we send them thank-you notes. The idea is to get new customers, keep those customers long term, and then get more new customers. The best direct marketers understand the importance of customer retention. That's why companies like American Express send a newsletter enclosed with their bill every month to let you know what's going on with the company along with new ways you can use your card. It's why other companies give special discounts to their best customers, keeping them loyal and encouraging them to buy more.

> *Direct marketers are continually looking for ways to add value to their product or service, keep their current customers happy, and get new customers coming in.*

Direct marketing is so effective that Fortune 500 companies are apportioning more and more of their budget to this area. Many small- and medium-size businesses are also jumping on the bandwagon and spending all of their advertising budget on direct marketing. Why?

> *Direct marketing is the easiest, most cost-effective way to form a relationship with your customer, and that is what brings in new customers and keeps current ones coming back.*

WHY DOES *YOUR* BUSINESS NEED DIRECT MARKETING?

Direct marketing is your best chance to get the edge over your competitors—large and small. Direct marketing is a great equalizer. You can run a million-dollar business out of a corner of your bedroom. You can give your product or service the same professional image that huge corporations give their products or services but without spending hundreds of thousands of dollars.

Direct marketing can introduce your business to thousands of customers who might otherwise never get the opportunity to shop from you. For instance, suppose a small bookstore located in Philadelphia, specializing in books for animal lovers, wants to broaden its customer base. Using direct marketing, this store can target pet owners throughout Pennsylvania or throughout the entire United States, reaching thousands more potential customers than it ever could through its lone retail outlet.

ASK DR. DIRECT . . .

"Why should I spend my hard-earned dollars on direct mail when I can place a beautiful display ad in my local newspaper?"

Direct marketing is an effective choice because:

☞ *You can reach a large universe of targeted customers.* You won't waste money on prospects who are not interested or qualified to purchase your product or use your service.

☞ *Direct marketing is the only advertising medium that is measurable.* You know exactly how many responses you get and where those responses come from.

☞ *Direct marketing puts you in control.* Because it is immediate and measurable (as opposed to regular advertising, which is used to build an image over time and does not produce a measurable response), you can use direct marketing to build your business when you need it most. For example, if March and April are normally quiet months, you can do a mailing in February that will bring you customers during the slow months.

☞ *Direct marketing is cost-efficient.* Even though your initial direct marketing effort, with all its up-front costs, may appear expensive, in the long run it's less expensive than any other kind of medium available.

☞ *Direct marketing fosters loyalty.* It costs much less to maintain a current customer than to bring in a new one. Direct marketing keeps you in contact with your customers, even when you don't have the time or money to stay in contact personally. Your cards and letters can make customers feel as if you're talking to them personally, which creates a strong bond customers are reluctant to break.

☞ *Direct marketing builds your customer list (database).* The more information you have about your customers, the more efficiently you can market to them. You can also use that information to search for prospects who match current customer profiles.

EVALUATING YOUR BUSINESS

You must ask yourself two main questions before you begin a direct marketing campaign:

> ► **What do I sell?**
>
> ► **Who are my customers?**

What do I sell?

When you begin considering direct marketing, you have to decide what it is that you want to sell. Are you selling a product? If so, you need to be able to answer these questions:

1. How would I describe this product to someone who has never seen anything like it?

2. How is this product different from others like it? (Is it of higher quality? Lower price? Does it "do more" or "do it better"?)

3. Why should someone buy it from me instead of buying it somewhere else?

Are you selling a service? Ask yourself these similar questions:

1. How would I describe my service to someone who has never used it before?

2. How is my service different from others like it? (Is it more convenient? Is it less expensive? Can I get it done faster?)

3. Why should someone use my service instead of going to someone else?

Who are my customers?

Do you know who your present customers are? Who are the people most likely to buy your product or service in the future? Take a few minutes and visualize your ideal customer. Don't try to visualize thousands of people; create an image of just one person. We call this your *target market*. If you're selling custom-made wedding gowns, your target market is obviously going to be different than if you are selling toy soldiers.

The idea is to get your message into the hands of as many people as possible who *want and need* your product or service now.

WHAT ARE YOUR MAIN REASONS FOR USING DIRECT MARKETING?

How have you promoted your products before?

Display ads ❑

Yellow Pages ❑

Public relations ❑

Word of mouth ❑

Other ❑

How have these efforts worked for you?

_____

_____

_____

_____

_____

_____

What do you want direct marketing to do for you?

_____

_____

_____

_____

_____

FINDING YOUR TARGET MARKET

ASK DR. DIRECT . . .

"How do I figure out who my ideal customer is?"

Five things to consider when visualizing your ideal customer:

☞ *Sex.* Does your product or service appeal more to men or women? Both?

☞ *Age.* Is your customer likely to be under 20? Over 50? Entering college? Reaching retirement? Somewhere in between?

☞ *Income.* If you're selling an expensive product or service, your customer probably needs an income level high enough to be able to afford what you're offering. You don't want to waste your time offering a $1,000 necklace to someone who can't afford to spend that much.

☞ *Psychographics.* This refers to the type of person who is likely to buy your product or service. For instance, it may be a product that will appeal to men who enjoy camping, or it may be a service that will appeal to women who are juggling career and family.

☞ *Mail Order Affinity.* People who have bought through the mail before are likely to do it again. What other things might these people have bought through the mail that would give them a high propensity to purchase your product or service?

TARGET MARKET WORKSHEET

Here's the scenario:

> You're the proud designer and manufacturer of Kids' Klubhouse, a kid-size clubhouse that comes in a kit parents can assemble for their kids to have "hours of imaginative, entertaining playtime." It sells for $50, plus shipping and handling. Who would be the ideal customer for this product? (See my answers at the bottom of the worksheet.)

Gender: _____

Age: _____

Income: _____

Psychographics: _____

Mail Order Affinity: _____

Who Is the Ideal Customer for Your Business?

Description of Business: _____

Gender: _____

Age: _____

Income: _____

Psychographics: _____

Mail Order Affinity: _____

OK, here are my answers:

Gender: Probably women, as they buy most children's products.

Age: There would probably be two categories: young mothers between the ages of 23 and 33 and grandmothers over 50.

Income: $35,000+.

Psychographics: They would probably be homeowners (to have room for the Klubhouse) with young children; possibly they would be busy working moms.

Mail Order Affinity: Bought toys and/or children's clothing through the mail.

DIRECT MARKETING FEASIBILITY

How do you know if direct marketing is practical for your company? What opportunities might it offer you? What might its drawbacks be? Here are some ideas to consider in determining if direct marketing is right for you.

Five things to think about when considering a direct marketing campaign:

1. *What will happen if you expand your business?*

Recently, a dentist came to me for advice about marketing his invention. It was a device to stop snoring that was implanted directly into the patient's mouth. The dentist was very excited about his product and wanted to implement a direct marketing campaign. My question was, "How are you going to sell all these devices when you're the only person who is currently equipped to implant them?" He finally realized that he had to begin by training other dentists to implant the device.

If you're selling a product, you have to think about how many items you can manufacture, store, and/or ship out if your business increases, and whether or not you will have to hire more people or enlarge your quarters to keep up with demand. You might want to start out with a limited campaign so that you can build your business slowly without overloading yourself or your resources.

2. *Figure out your capacity to service customers and then work backwards.*

The dentist might only be able to service 50 new patients himself. How many direct mail pieces does he need to mail in order to get 50 new customers? Because the average response to any mailing is 1–2%, he needs to mail out at least 5,000 letters.

3. *Establish what you can afford to pay to get a new customer.*

If you're selling a product and your goal is to get 500 new orders, you would need to mail out 50,000 letters. If it costs you $1 for each mailing piece, you'll be spending $50,000. What is your return for 500 new customers? If it's less than $50,000, direct mail may not be the way to go. (Direct response advertising may give you a better return—see Part IV.)

DIRECT MARKETING FEASIBILITY
(continued)

4. *Determine the cost of your product vs. the cost of mailing it out.*

Another man came to me with a barbecue grill he wanted to sell through the mail. It was a high-quality product that would appeal to a large number of people. His goal was to sell 5,000 grills the first year. His selling price was $200. However, he hadn't taken the weight of the grill into consideration. It was over the weight limit for most commercial shippers. He would have had to hire a private shipper at a cost of almost $100 per grill. He discovered it was not feasible to sell his product through the mail.

5. *Do some "grass-roots" research.*

Take your product around; show it to people. Let them use it. Ask them what they think of it. If you perform a service, do it for people for free or at a reduced price. Get an evaluation of what you do or what you offer. If a competitor is already offering what you have, you should know about it. If there are unique qualities that prospective customers really appreciate, you should know about that, too.

P A R T

II

Planning Your Direct Marketing Campaign

STEP 1: CLARIFY YOUR OBJECTIVES

Here's a scenario I run into all the time:

1. John Doe of Acme Widgets Incorporated has decided to try direct marketing for his new Super Widget.

2. He calls a meeting of his vice presidents, announces his intentions, and asks for their input. VP#1 says, "Great idea! Let's have a contest to promote Super Widgets!"

3. VP#2 says, "Wonderful plan! Why don't we put an ad in the paper and have people send in coupons for sample Super Widgets."

4. And VP#3 says, "Let's think big: a half-hour infomercial with Tiger Woods as our spokesperson!"

John Doe and his VPs are making the same mistake most people make when they consider direct marketing—they're deciding on tactics (how they're going to carry out the campaign) before they have a clear picture of what they're trying to accomplish.

Before you start to think about *how* you're going to conduct your direct marketing campaign, you must be sure you know *what you want it to do* for you. What are your objectives? If you own a retail store, your objective might be to build store traffic during normally slow months. For any type of business, service, or product, your objective might be to build a database (or customer file), with specific information that will allow you to target special offers to particular customers. Or your objective might be to introduce a new product or service nationwide.

The first step in planning your campaign is to make a list of your objectives. It's possible to have more than one objective, but it's important to determine your primary objective and keep the focus on that. Your objectives should be concise and specific, including dollar figures, percentages, and/or time lines whenever possible.

Here is an example of a poor objective: *to increase sales.* Here is a better version: *to increase sales by 25% by the third quarter of next year.* Including specific percentages, numbers, and dates makes it easier to determine whether or not you've met your objectives.

OBJECTIVES WORKSHEET

What do you really want to achieve, and when? Check off each item that applies. I want to:

- ❏ Increase my bottom line

- ❏ Generate leads that can later be converted to sales

- ❏ Increase store traffic or number of clients

- ❏ Establish and/or build my customer list

- ❏ Test various lists and/or offers to see which gets the best response

My specific objectives (including numbers, percentages, and dates) are:

_____

_____

_____

_____

STEP 2: CHOOSE YOUR STRATEGY

Once you know your objective, you have to figure out what "big idea" you will use to meet your goal. Suppose you own a retail store, and your objective is to increase customer flow by 30% during the normally slow month of July. Your strategy might be to do a special mailing campaign inviting customers to come in to its store for the "Fourth of July Month-Long Sales Bonanza." Another strategy might to be to develop a contest with a four-part entry form—one for each week in July. The idea is to zero in on the "big things" you can do to achieve your goals.

Your choice of strategy will be based on your:

- Objectives

- Budget

- Product or service

- Time limitations

- Target audience

Three Examples of Strategies

► You design and manufacture collectible dolls. Your objective is to sell 1,000 dolls in the next six months. Your strategy might be to design a limited-edition line, signed and numbered, and available only until Christmas Eve 1999. Or your strategy might be, like that used by the Cabbage Patch Kids dolls, to give each doll a name and personal history, and provide adoption papers for new "parents."

► You manufacture and distribute audio books-on-tape. Your objective is to build your customer base by 35% by the third quarter of next year. Your strategy might be to develop a book club in which members can get special offers and large discounts and earn points toward free cassettes.

► You are an accountant moving your office to a new location. Your objective is to bring in 30 new clients by April 15 of next year. Your strategy might be to target a direct mail campaign to people within a five-mile radius of your office with an income of $40,000+ by announcing a series of free seminars to answer the most frequently asked tax questions.

CAMPAIGN STRATEGY WORKSHEET

► Remember, the strategy is the "big idea" for your direct marketing campaign.

► Design your strategy with your ideal customer in mind. What would make that customer respond?

► Differentiate yourself from the competition. If your "rival" is offering discount prices and warehouse sales, do something completely different. Give customers a reason to do business with *you*.

Strategy #1: _____

_____

_____

_____

_____

Strategy #2: _____

_____

_____

_____

_____

Strategy #3: _____

_____

_____

_____

_____

STEP 3: CHOOSE YOUR TACTICS

The next phase of planning your campaign is to decide how you are going to implement your strategy. Tactics are the little things that make your strategies happen. Tactics are the fun part; they are the things people spend most of their time on, when they should be spending time on strategies. Deciding on tactics means making creative choices about how an ad is going to look, what kind of paper a letter is going to be printed on, and how a product will be presented to the public. This is where you finally get to create specific ideas for implementing your campaign.

Your budget is your main consideration when you figure out your tactics. It will set the parameters for the kind of tactics you choose. If you have a small budget, you may want to try some small space ads in magazines and newspapers. A larger budget may allow you to go with a direct mail campaign. If you have an even larger budget, you may want to try direct response television. You will have lots of tactical decisions to make once you decide on a program. Whichever program you decide on will be made up of various components. All of those components are a part of your tactics.

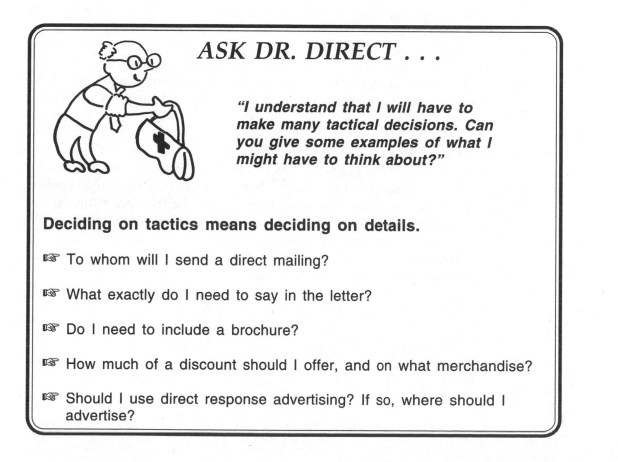

ASK DR. DIRECT . . .

"I understand that I will have to make many tactical decisions. Can you give some examples of what I might have to think about?"

Deciding on tactics means deciding on details.

☞ To whom will I send a direct mailing?

☞ What exactly do I need to say in the letter?

☞ Do I need to include a brochure?

☞ How much of a discount should I offer, and on what merchandise?

☞ Should I use direct response advertising? If so, where should I advertise?

STEP 3: CHOOSE YOUR TACTICS (continued)

Three Examples of Tactics

The following three examples describe tactics you might employ to carry out the three strategies outlined in the previous section. Use the worksheet that follows to create a set of tactics suitable to *your* objectives and strategies.

▶ You design and manufacture collectible dolls. Your objective is to sell 1,000 dolls in the next six months. Your strategy might be to design a limited-edition line, signed and numbered, and available only until Christmas Eve 1999. Your tactics might include sending a direct mail package including a letter, a four-color brochure, and a business reply envelope to a list of people who have ordered other collectibles through the mail. Another tactic is to state that if they order a doll before November 1, 1999, they will receive free an additional dress-up outfit for the doll.

▶ You manufacture and distribute audio books-on-tape. Your objective is to build your customer base by 35% by the third quarter of next year. Your strategy might be to develop a book club where members can get special offers and large discounts and earn points toward free cassettes. Your tactic might be to place small ads in several literary and travel-oriented magazines, giving your 800 number for people to call for your membership brochure.

▶ You are an accountant moving your office to a new location. Your objective is to bring in 30 new clients by April 15 of next year. Your strategy might be to hold a series of free seminars to answer the most frequently asked tax questions. Your tactic might be to send a formal invitation to residents within a five-mile radius of your new office announcing your move and the time, date, and location of your free seminars. You also might want to offer those who attend a free booklet outlining important tax tips for the coming year.

CAMPAIGN TACTICS WORKSHEET

Tactic #1: _____

_____

_____

_____

_____

Tactic #2: _____

_____

_____

_____

_____

Tactic #3: _____

_____

_____

_____

_____

STEP 4: DESIGN A MARKETING PLAN

Direct marketing can be as simple as mailing postcards to your best customers thanking them for their recent purchases and offering them a brand-new product, or as complicated as mailing 1 million four-color packages that include seven different components and a free sample. But even the simplest campaigns require organization, planning, and forethought. The best way to accomplish this is to put together a direct marketing plan you can follow—and refer back to—as your campaign unfolds.

Your plan should contain seven areas of pertinent information in order to make it successful:

1. **BACKGROUND:** This section includes a description of your product or service and a short history of your company. It might also include a *competitive analysis*, a description of how your product or service differs from and is superior to other products or services similar to yours.

This section should also include any other marketing programs you have tested in the past, and their results. I once worked on a campaign with a client who didn't tell me that he'd already tried a direct marketing campaign. He waited until I'd designed my own campaign, and then told me he'd already tested a similar program. Even if you're directing your own campaign, it's a good idea to refresh your memory and include everything you've tested before.

2. **OBJECTIVES:** Describe what you really want to achieve with your direct marketing campaign, including as much specific information as possible.

3. **STRATEGY:** This is the "big idea" that takes you from your objective to your tactics. Remember to keep in mind your budget, your time limitations, and your target market.

4. **TACTICS:** Exactly how are you going to implement your strategy? For every strategy, there's at least one tactic. Tactics are the action steps that accomplish the strategy.

5. **BALLPARK ESTIMATES:** It's one thing to design a direct marketing campaign that includes all the things you'd really like to do. It's another thing to find out exactly how much everything will cost. Your plan should include estimates for every detail you've outlined in your tactics. If you're planning to send out a direct mail package with an outer envelope, a letter, a brochure, an order form, and a business reply card, you have to know what each of those components will cost. If you're planning to use direct response advertising, you'll need to know what it costs to place an ad in each publication you're considering. Once you've determined what all of these costs will be, you can then figure out what the response rate has to be in order to realize a profit.

6. **CONTINGENCY PLANS:** Include several "what if" scenarios in your plan. What if the mailing doesn't produce the expected response? What will your next step be? What if the mailing produces a greater-than-expected response? What if one ad pulls in a much greater response than all the others do? If you already have these "what if" situations spelled out, you won't have to make last-minute decisions later on. The most important "what if" is what if your test does very well—what are your next steps? If you've used a small portion of a large mailing list, can you "roll it out," or mail to the rest of the people on the list? How quickly can you accomplish that? Should you use the same offer or try a different one?

7. **TIMETABLE:** This is another instance where you need to work backwards. If you know you want to place an ad in the October issue of a certain magazine, you must call that magazine and find out the closing date (the last date on which they will accept materials) for that issue. If the closing date is August 15, then you know you must start several weeks before then in order to get the concept and design work done. All deadlines need to be noted and marked on everyone's calendars.

DIRECT MARKETING PLAN WORKSHEET

1. *BACKGROUND:* _____
_____
_____
_____
_____
_____

2. *OBJECTIVES:* _____
_____
_____
_____
_____
_____

3. *STRATEGY:* _____
_____
_____
_____
_____
_____

4. *TACTICS:* _____
_____
_____
_____
_____
_____

5. *BALLPARK ESTIMATES:* _____
_____
_____
_____
_____
_____

6. *CONTINGENCY PLANS:* _____
_____
_____
_____
_____
_____

7. *TIMETABLE:* _____
_____
_____
_____
_____
_____

P A R T

III

Creating a Direct Mail Package

ELEMENTS OF A DIRECT MAIL PACKAGE

When you open your mailbox, what do you see? If you're like most people, you receive one or two personal letters, a few bills, a catalog or two, and several direct mail packages that contain solicitations for you to purchase a product or service. Unlike general advertising, which expects you to take action at some later time, the purpose of direct mail is to get you to make out a check or call the 800 number and order *right now*.

There is one distinct disadvantage to direct mail: it is relatively expensive. So why is it used so often? Because it works. Here are some reasons why:

▶ **A TARGETED AUDIENCE:** If you're a smart marketer who has put together a good plan, you know that you're sending your mailing to people who are likely to have an interest in your product. If you put an ad in the paper or on television, it's difficult to know just who you are reaching.

▶ **MEASURABILITY:** When you use direct mail, you choose your lists of prospective customers for specific reasons. You know exactly how many people will be receiving your package and just who they are. When people respond, you can keep track of them and what list they came from. That way, you'll know which lists to use again (or to expand) the next time you want to send a mailing.

▶ **TIMELINESS:** Most people look forward to getting their mail and open it as soon as it arrives. An effective outer envelope can get a prospective customer to open the direct mail package immediately.

▶ **CREATIVITY:** Direct mail gives you more creative freedom than most other forms of advertising. You have neither the space limitations of print advertising nor the time limitations of broadcast advertising. As long as your budget allows, you can send just about anything in a direct mail package.

▶ **GROWTH POSSIBILITIES:** One of the best things about direct mail is that you can start small and grow at your own pace. If you rent a mailing list of 5,000 names (the usual minimum), you don't have to send the mailing all at once. Spread it out over time. You can begin your efforts out of your home office or garage and expand slowly along with your business.

ELEMENTS OF A DIRECT MAIL PACKAGE
(continued)

A direct mail package can be large or small. It can be a simple letter or a complex package containing five or six pieces. Most direct mail packages include one or more of the following elements:

1. **The Outer Envelope**

2. **The Letter**

3. **The Brochure**

4. **The Lift Letter**

5. **The Order Form**

6. **The Business Reply Card or Envelope**

7. **The Catalog**

1. THE OUTER ENVELOPE

Direct marketers often put in long hours drafting a letter, designing a brochure, and creating an effective order form. They tend to ignore the outer envelope. But the outer envelope is what first gets a potential customer's attention. The envelope's main purpose is to get someone to open it. There might be 10 or 15 (or in my case 40) different pieces of mail in a customer's box on any given day. Your envelope will be competing with other direct mail, as well as catalogs and magazines. It has to make a strong statement and stand out from the crowd. Here are seven ways to get your envelope noticed:

- *Make the envelope look as though a human being has touched it.* Mail it to a real person—not "Resident, Apt. 8A." If possible, check to see that spellings are correct. If you can, put the personalized name and address directly on the envelope, as opposed to on a label that gets affixed to the envelope.

- *Use a* **live** *stamp.* That's an industry term for a regular stamp, not a postage-machine indicia. You can get third-class stamps (or a mailing house can put them on for you). Or if you're doing a small mailing and can afford it, buy interesting first-class stamps. With so many categories from which to choose now, you can probably find one that relates to your product. For instance, if you are selling children's toys, you might want to choose a Bugs Bunny stamp; if you are selling movie memorabilia, a Marilyn Monroe stamp would be perfect. Another hint is to use more than one stamp. If you're doing a small mailing or a mailing in several waves, putting two or three stamps on the envelope can work well. It gives it an added human touch, as large mailers usually don't do that kind of thing.

- *Include a teaser line on the envelope.* You've probably seen teasers like the following: "Free Recipe Book, See Inside." Or "Think you can't eat ice cream and French fries and still lose weight? Open this envelope and find out the surprising answer!" Don't give away the whole story, but try something that will pique readers' interest and make them curious enough to open your envelope.

- *Use color and graphics.* If you're selling a "glamour" product, you might want to show it right on the envelope. I once designed a campaign for *Better Homes and Gardens* to sell a book on quilting. The outer envelope featured a beautiful full-color photograph of one of the quilts. Quilters loved it, and the campaign was a great success. If you can't afford full color, you might try a black-and-white illustration. Anything to jazz up the envelope and make it interesting.

1. THE OUTER ENVELOPE (continued)

- *Utilize both sides of the envelope.* Try putting your teaser on the reverse side of an envelope. If you can do it with a sense of humor, so much the better.

- *Include your return address.* If the mailing cannot be delivered, you want to know about it so you can remove the name from your list. Another technique that can sometimes lift the response rate is to put your initials in script (you can handwrite it for a small mailing, or use a computer script font on a larger one) above the return address so it looks like it has come from a real person. Sometimes, though, it's a good idea to test a mailing with no return address, because it makes people curious about where the letter came from.

- *Try elegant simplicity.* Perhaps your product or service doesn't call for a "loud" introduction. If you're offering a professional service, for instance, you might want to go with a plain white envelope with a live stamp on it. The more it looks like a personal letter, the more likely people will open it immediately.

How to Use Third-Class Mail

Let the post office know you're planning a large mailing. If possible, take a copy of the mailing over to your local postmaster and ask if there are any regulations you need to meet. Always check with your post office to be sure your mail meets all government regulations.

► **If you mail anything other than standard-size envelopes, you will pay an additional fee.** Minimum standard-size envelopes are at least $3\,^1/_2$" × 5". The largest standard-size envelope is $6\,^1/_8$" × $11\,^1/_2$".

► **Direct mail advertising is usually sent third class.** First class is for business and personal mail; second class is for periodicals; third class is for direct mail advertising; and fourth class is for parcels.

► **Ask your post office for your free copy of the publication *Third-Class Mail Preparation.*** It will tell you the regulations you need to follow.

► **If you use a mailing house or lettershop (a facility that does all the preparation necessary to get direct mail to the post office and into homes of recipients), they will prepare your mail according to government regulations.**

1. THE OUTER ENVELOPE (continued)

Here are two successful outer envelopes:

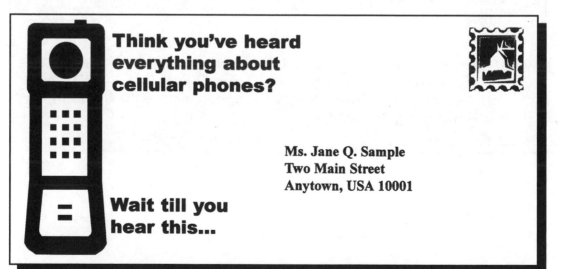

2. THE LETTER

The letter is the most important element of your direct mail campaign. It sets the tone for the whole package. The letter is like the salesperson who goes house to house to sell your product. Here are 10 steps toward creating an effective direct mail letter:

STEP #1

Humanize your letter. It should sound like it was written by a real person—from one human being to another, not from a company to a person. Think about letters you've gotten from family and friends. They tell a story, they let you know what's happening, they urge you to "keep in touch." Your direct mail letter should do the same.

STEP #2

Avoid the "fourth-paragraph disease." Draft the entire letter and include everything you want to say. Then go back and reread it. Usually, you'll find you can eliminate the first three paragraphs. The fourth paragraph often gets to the meat of the matter.

STEP #3

Make the letter long enough to tell your whole story. People often think a letter should be no longer than one page. Not true. It has to be as long as necessary to tell the whole story. If your product or service is complicated or contains several elements, a three- or four-page letter, or even longer, might be appropriate. If what you're selling is self-explanatory, a one-pager may be all you need. Don't predetermine the length. Keep writing until you've said everything. Then go back and edit until the letter says everything that needs to be said but no more. Show it to several people to get their feedback.

STEP #4

Use interesting letterhead. Spend some time designing letterhead that represents your company. The style should match your company's style. If your company is down-home and friendly, use an informal typeface. If you want to represent a more professional image, then a more corporate-looking design might be right for you. Be sure to include all pertinent information, including your name, title, company name, address, phone and fax numbers, and your e-mail address.

2. THE LETTER (continued)

Personalize your salutation. If it's possible, use the prospect's name instead of "Dear Friend." For a small mailing, that's easy enough to do with any word processing software. If you're doing a large mailing through a mailing house, they can do it for you (for a fee, of course). If you don't know the names of your prospect, address them by a relevant category name such as "Dear Busy Mom," Dear Club Member," or Dear Cat Lover." Another choice is to make the salutation the beginning of a sentence. For example:

It's as simple as this, dear friend,

   If you want to save time and money, I have just the product for you.

STEP #6

Include a Johnson box. This is an attention-getter that's placed at the top of the letter before the salutation. It can be used to introduce a special offer, emphasize an important benefit, or tease the prospect into reading the rest of the letter. It can also be a testimonial from a satisfied customer. And it doesn't always have to be contained in a box. It can be a cartoon or illustration, and it can be printed in another color ink or stuck on a Post-it note. Here is an example:

Mr. John Q. Sample
One Main Street
Anytown, USA 10001

> Read on and find out how to get a beautiful bouquet of colorful wildflowers, worth $24.95, delivered FREE right to your home!

Dear Mr. Sample:

STEP #7

Use crossheads. Crossheads are boldfaced or underlined subheads that appear in between certain paragraphs. They break up the monotonous rhythm of one paragraph after another and keep your eye moving along. Break up the type by making some words bold and underlining others. You can also use different typefaces. Don't go overboard, though. Most text is easier to read with a typeface that has serifs (the little lines that appear at the tops and bottoms of letters). Newspapers generally use serif type because it's easier to read when there is a lot of text. Sans serif type is good for headlines.

This is a typeface with serifs.
This is a typeface without serifs.

Use bullets to show benefits and important points. Even if people don't read your letter word for word, they will scan for things that jump out at them.

STEP #8

Include a call to action. Tell people what you want them to do. "Order by September 22 to get your FREE gift." "Send in your order today." "Spend $60 or more, and take 15% off your order." The idea is to say, "Do It Now." The last line of your letter should include the call to action.

STEP #9

Sign your letter in blue ink. It may not be possible to sign all the letters yourself, but there are ways to scan in your signature so that each letter looks hand signed. Even though people usually realize that you didn't sign each letter personally, this technique almost always lifts response.

STEP #10

Include a P.S. People often read the end of a letter first (to see who sent it), so the P.S. can really catch their attention. This is a good place to reiterate your offer, or even to make an offer that was not included in the body of the letter.

2. THE LETTER (continued)

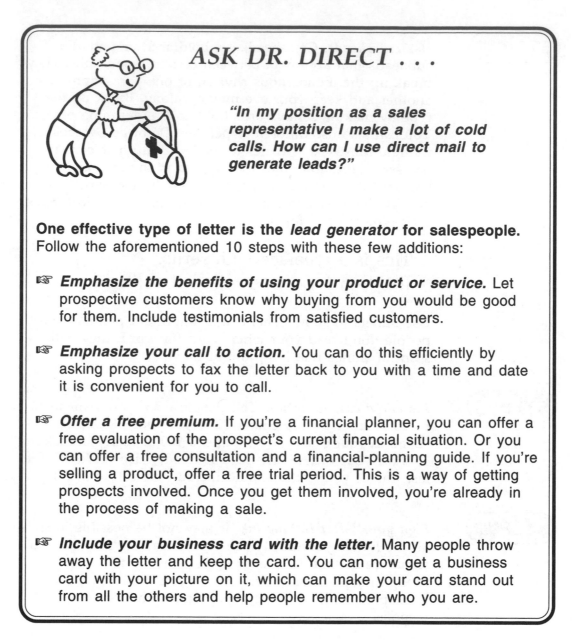

ASK DR. DIRECT . . .

"In my position as a sales representative I make a lot of cold calls. How can I use direct mail to generate leads?"

One effective type of letter is the *lead generator* for salespeople. Follow the aforementioned 10 steps with these few additions:

☞ *Emphasize the benefits of using your product or service.* Let prospective customers know why buying from you would be good for them. Include testimonials from satisfied customers.

☞ *Emphasize your call to action.* You can do this efficiently by asking prospects to fax the letter back to you with a time and date it is convenient for you to call.

☞ *Offer a free premium.* If you're a financial planner, you can offer a free evaluation of the prospect's current financial situation. Or you can offer a free consultation and a financial-planning guide. If you're selling a product, offer a free trial period. This is a way of getting prospects involved. Once you get them involved, you're already in the process of making a sale.

☞ *Include your business card with the letter.* Many people throw away the letter and keep the card. You can now get a business card with your picture on it, which can make your card stand out from all the others and help people remember who you are.

Here are two successful direct mail letters:

January 26, 1998

Mr. John Doe
President
Acme Office Supplies
1 Main Street
Anytown, USA   12345

Dear Mr. Doe,

I'll be quick.

If you'll spend 30 minutes talking to my creative director and me
about direct marketing . . .

. . . we'll spend three solid hours working on your business. Then
we'll come back to you with ideas—ideas that can create incremental
revenue for Acme Office Supplies.

At the very least, you'll get the recommendations of two outside
experts to think about early in 1998.

I'll follow up in a few days to see if you're willing to invest the
30 minutes. I'm certainly ready to invest the three hours of our time.

Thanks for reading this.

Sincerely,

Lois Geller

P.S. I've always wanted to talk to you about loyalty marketing . . . and
bonding your good customers so tightly to Acme Office Supplies that
they wouldn't dream of going anywhere else.

2. THE LETTER (continued)

June 3, 1998

Ms. Lois Geller
54 Elm Street
Springvale, IL 23245

We want to meet you! Special introductory offer for all new patients. Call us today for a complete dental examination—only $65.00!

Dear Ms. Geller,

Let me introduce myself.

My name is Richard Green, D.D.S. I've just moved here from Chicago, where I had a busy practice for over seven years. Last year my wife, Ellen (who is also my dental hygienist), and I decided we wanted to trade in the hustle and bustle of city life for a quieter, calmer atmosphere in which to raise our two young sons, Bradley and John.

As soon as we saw Springvale, we knew this was the place for us.

Springvale offers us the lifestyle we've always dreamt about. And we now offer all our neighbors in Springvale high-quality, affordable personal dental care, including:

- State-of-the-art equipment and sterilization techniques
- Evening and weekend appointments
- Senior-citizen and student discounts
- Acceptance by most insurance plans

Please come in and see us in our offices at the corner of Park and Third. Take advantage of our new-patient welcoming offer. For only $65 you'll receive:

- A complete dental exam
- Oral-cancer screening
- A thorough cleaning
- Any necessary X-rays
- A consultation

We're looking forward to meeting you.

Sincerely,

Dr. Richard Green

3. THE BROCHURE

It is not always necessary to send a brochure with your direct mail package. If you're marketing your financial-planning services, you probably don't need a brochure. But if you want or need to show off your product, a brochure is the best way to go. Suppose you are marketing a Swiss Army–type knife with many different tools attached (such as scissors, a nail file, a screwdriver, etc.). You'll need to do more than just explain how the knife works. You'll need to demonstrate all the wonderful things you can do with just this one purchase.

Here are seven tips on how to create a terrific brochure:

 Include all your ordering information in the brochure. The brochure often gets separated from the rest of the direct mail package. People often take the brochure and put it in their purse or wallet so they can show it to others or peruse it at their leisure. If there's no ordering information, you may lose the sale.

TIP #2 ***Use headlines with full sentences.*** And make them action oriented, like "Don't Be Caught Unprepared. Our All-Purpose Knife Is the Only Tool You'll Ever Need!"

TIP #3 ***Use "lifestyle" photographs.*** People like to look at people, so be sure to include them in your photos. Show people demonstrating your product, using your product, having a good life as a result of using your product. Think of it this way: when you come back from your vacation with 12 photos of Niagara Falls, it's the one with Uncle Harry standing in front of the falls that you're going to keep. And if you're including a free gift or premium with your offer, show a photograph of that as well.

3. THE BROCHURE (continued)

Know the difference between features and benefits. People don't actually buy products—they buy the things products can do for them. All products and services have two components: features and benefits. Features describe what the product or service is. The All-Purpose Knife is a multi-faceted tool that contains a knife, scissors, a nail file, a toothpick, a mini-screwdriver, etc. Those are the product's features. Would I buy this knife? Not until I know how it will benefit me. I'll buy the knife if you tell me: "This knife is impossible to lose, as it's made of glow-in-the-dark, luminescent plastic. It's so small it will fit in any pocket, yet so versatile it can be used for hundreds of household, craft, and outdoor jobs." Knowing the benefits entices me to buy this product.

Include captions or callouts with all your photographs. Marketing studies have shown that captions and callouts are among the most-read areas of any brochure. Callouts are those little lines or arrows that point out a specific feature of the product. Callouts can simply name the feature, but captions should be full sentences and action oriented.

Use color. Most people use color in photographs only. But if you're paying for a four-color printing job, take full advantage of the possibilities. Use a tint behind the type. Use a border around the brochure to give it added interest. Even if you're using only two colors, you can use various shades of color to add highlights and contrast.

Keep the folds in mind. Make a mock version of your brochure and how you want it to fold. Put it in an envelope and see how it unfolds when you take it out. You'll be wasting money if parts of your product are hidden in the folds.

The Lift Letter

The lift letter was originally called the *publisher's letter* because it started in the publishing industry. The main letter would be signed by the director of circulation, and a smaller letter, with the headline "If you decide not to buy this product, please open this," was signed by the publisher himself. The lift letter is usually written in a very down-to-earth, easy tone. It reiterates the benefits of the product or service. The lift letter isn't necessary, but many marketers have found that these letters lift response.

Here's an example of an effective lift letter:

If you're hesitating about ordering now . . .

I recently went on a camping trip up in the mountains. Everything that could have gone wrong went wrong. It poured for three days. We couldn't get the tent up. We lost a sleeping bag but found the poison ivy. The one saving grace was the All-Purpose Knife that I had casually dropped in my pocket on my way out the door. When Johnny got popcorn stuck in his tooth, the toothpick helped us out. When the fishing lines got hopelessly tangled, the knife cut right through them. The All-Purpose Knife saved our camping trip. We'll never go camping without it! And you shouldn't either.

Sincerely,

Robert Smith
President, Acme Corporation

P.S. Don't forget, it makes a great gift, too. Don't miss out on this great offer. Return the order form today.

5. THE ORDER FORM

Whether you call it a reply card, a reservation form, or a trial certificate, the order form should be a mini-ad for your product or service. It should include your most important sales points. You order form should stand on its own as an effective selling tool. Here are some tips on how to accomplish this goal:

▶ *Start the order form with a "YES!"* Then continue with "I would like to order the All-Purpose Knife at the one-time-only price of $29.95. If I am not completely satisfied, I can return the knife within 30 days for a full refund."

▶ *Include a guarantee.* Every direct marketing campaign should include a guarantee. People need to be reassured that if they make a mistake in ordering, they can change their minds.

▶ *Make sure you have spaces for people to fill in all pertinent information.* Make the lines long enough so people with long names can fit their entire name. Ask for phone numbers and e-mail addresses, so that if there are any problems you can contact them.

▶ *Give people payment options.* If you accept checks, let people know to whom the checks should be made out. If you accept credit cards, leave spaces for the credit card number, the expiration date, and the customer's signature. Be sure to let customers know about shipping-and-handling charges, and whether or not they have to pay sales tax.

▶ *Make your order form interesting.* Give people incentive to buy from you. Make it fun to order! Use color, graphics, cartoon characters. If you want people to cut the order form out, include a little scissors logo (✄) and "cut here" instructions. For some reason, this always lifts response.

▶ *Use an involvement device.* If you can afford it, include peel-off stickers that say "yes," "no," or "maybe," which customers can pull off your letter or brochure and stick on the order form. Why would you want a "no" or a "maybe"? If people are involved enough to move the stickers, it means they're just a little interested. If people respond with a "no," put them in your database and write to them again later. People who respond with a "maybe" are very close to buying. They might have a question or an objection. You can either solicit them again soon, or you can call them and ask why they chose not to buy at this time.

▶ *Include a source code.* If you're doing a large mailing, you've probably gotten your names from a number of different list sources. You want to know which of these lists is giving you the best results. Be sure to code each one so you'll know exactly where each of your orders is coming from.

▶ *Include a receipt.* You can often increase your response rate by including both a guarantee and a receipt on your order form (see below). This way, customers can keep a record of what they've ordered.

Here is an example of an effective order form:

Sample Order Form

Guarantee	YES! I want to order the All-Purpose Knife at the low introductory price of only $39.95.
If you are not 100% satisfied with your All-Purpose Knife, return it to us within 30 days for a full refund . . . no questions asked.	Please send me _____ knives at $39.95 $ _____ Shipping and handling 4.00 Sales tax (NY and OH residents) _____ Total enclosed $ _____ My check is enclosed, payable to: All-Purpose Knife, Inc. Please charge my: ❏ Visa ❏ Mastercard ❏ AMEX Acct. # _____ Exp. Date _____ Signature: _____ Name: _____ Address: _____ City: _____ State: _____ Zip: _____ Daytime phone: ( ) _____ **The All-Purpose Knife Company** **1-800-555-1234** **201 2nd Ave., Sioux Falls, SD 57117**

_____ _____ _____ Place Stamp Here	**Receipt** Order: All Purpose Knife Date: _____ Check #: _____
MAIL TO: The All Purpose Knife Company 201 2nd Avenue Sioux Falls, SD 57117	**NO-RISK 30 Day Money Back Guarantee** The All Purpose Knife Company **1-800-555-1234**

6. THE BUSINESS REPLY
ENVELOPE OR CARD

The easier you make if for prospective customers to send in their order, the more likely they are to do that. If you include a business reply envelope, people don't have to search for their own. If you can afford it, make the envelope prepaid so the customer does not have to provide the stamp.

If you do include a prepaid envelope:

1. You must obtain a permit and permit number from the United States Postal Service. There are stringent regulations that apply to business reply cards and envelopes, so be sure to check with your post office or mailing house.

2. The post office does give you some leeway. For instance, you can add in an address line like "Best Buy of the Year Department."

3. On the back of the envelope or on the inside flap, you might want to print a checklist for customers, with questions such as "Have you signed and enclosed your check?" and "Have you included your order form?"

4. Instead of a business reply envelope, you might want to include a business reply card. Cards are usually used for information ("fill in this card for your free information packet") rather than for ordering. Customers do not want to send their credit card numbers through the mail if anyone can read them.

7. THE CATALOG

There is so much to say about putting a catalog together, we couldn't possibly cover the whole subject in just a few pages. But because more than *14 billion* catalogs are mailed in the United States every year, we didn't want to ignore them either. Catalogs are a logical extension of direct marketing. As soon as you sell a customer one product, you have a likely customer for a follow-up product, or what we call a *line extension*. When you have enough of these products, it's time to put together a catalog.

Here are seven basics to keep in mind as you consider creating a catalog:

- *Give your catalog personality.* With so many catalogs out there, you must make yours memorable. You can do this by specializing in a particular type of merchandise (there's one catalog called "Cats, Cats, Cats," for instance, that features everything a cat lover could possibly desire). Or your style (homespun, extra elegant, country, urban sophisticate, etc.) can distinguish you from others with similar merchandise.

- *The outside cover is your display window.* The catalog should be looked upon as a mini-store, with every single part of it considered valuable real estate. The outside cover is the most valuable piece of all. It's the thing that's going to bring your customers in. The cover should feature your product in a lifestyle or other interesting shot. It should also let customers know what they are going to find in the catalog. Study magazine covers and note how they tell you (in short, enticing sentences) about the stories you'll find inside. Your catalog should do the same: "For great summer wear, see page 87," or "Take advantage of our special sale on silver earrings. See page 20 for details."

- *Address your customers personally.* The inside front cover should feature a letter to your customers from you or someone else in your company. This letter acts as your salesperson. It should have a sincere, warm feeling to it, establishing the human connection that is often missing from shopping by mail. This is your opportunity to share your ideas and philosophy with your customers and to let them in on specially featured items in the catalog.

- *Feature your lead products on the right-hand inside page.* This page usually lets customers know what kind of merchandise they can expect in the rest of the catalog. It also establishes the tone for the rest of the pages.

7. THE CATALOG (continued)

- *The center spread usually contains the order form.* Sometimes it appears at the end of the catalog. Wherever you place the order form, your best-sellers should surround it. When people turn to the order form, they naturally focus on the items nearby. Follow the tips for creating interesting order forms listed on pages 44–45; make sure you include all necessary information to make it easy for your customers to order from you.

- *The back page is a premium spot.* When people pull the catalog out of the mailbox, they may see the back cover first. So it has to be just as appealing and enticing as the front cover. It should also feature one of your hottest items.

- *Tell a story about each product in the catalog.* Don't just list the item, its features, and its price. Let your customers know how they can use the product, what the benefits are, why they will absolutely love this product and can't live without it. It's amazing how much you can do in a few short sentences.

Catalog Rules of Thumb

► **Start out small.** A large catalog is extremely complicated to put together. Figure out what merchandise you really want to include.

► **Make sure the items you want to include can be photographed effectively.** Some items are difficult to photograph, such as small, shiny objects. You might make some test photos yourself so that you can see what a professional photographer will be facing.

► **Show people how to fill out your order form.** Use the first line to show customers how to fill out the form (including item numbers, sizes, colors, quantity, etc.). Don't get too complicated with the tax and shipping-and-handling charges. If necessary, you can pay these charges yourself, rather than lose a customer who's sent the wrong amount. Be sure to include a "Ship To" option so that customers can ship gifts to friends or relatives.

P A R T

IV

How To Use Direct Response Advertising

DIRECT RESPONSE ADS

When you send a direct mail package to prospective customers, you already have their attention, to one degree or another. They have to look at the envelope and make a decision about it. It is hoped that they will open the envelope and read the letter, the brochure, and the order form. You have several chances to describe your product, list the benefits, and get your readers to buy. With a *direct response ad,* all you've got is a few seconds to get their attention before they turn the page.

And you're not only competing with the other ads in the newspaper or magazine, you're also competing with the publication's editorial content. A direct response ad, designed to generate an immediate response via mail or telephone, has to:

- Get readers' attention immediately

- Include benefits directly related to them

- Contain a great offer that will entice them to pick up the phone and order right away . . . all before they turn the page

Components of an Effective Ad

The main advantage of a direct response ad is that you can reach a large number of people for a smaller amount of money than it takes to put together a direct mail campaign or produce a catalog. There are fewer steps involved and fewer decisions to be made. Often, first-time direct marketers are advised to start by placing small direct response ads in several different publications, evaluating the responses, and using them to build their own databases.

There are four main components to a direct response ad:

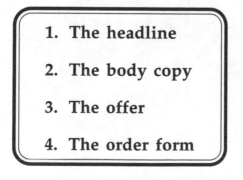

1. **The headline**

2. **The body copy**

3. **The offer**

4. **The order form**

THE HEADLINE

**MY ATTENTION-GRABBING HEADLINES
IN THE YELLOW PAGES INCREASED
MY BUSINESS BY 57%!**

**WOULDN'T YOU LIKE YOUR AD TO ATTRACT
THOUSANDS OF PROSPECTIVE CUSTOMERS?**

**"MY WHOLE STAFF THOUGHT IT WAS HILARIOUS
WHEN I PUT A SMALL CLASSIFIED AD WITH A CATCHY
HEADLINE IN THE *NEW YORK TIMES* . . . UNTIL WE
RECEIVED 43 NEW PROSPECTS IN ONE WEEK!"**

—Sandy Simpson, La Jolla, CA

If you read any of the three headlines above, wouldn't they catch your eye? Wouldn't they make you want to read on? Headlines have one major purpose: to grab readers' attention and keep them from turning the page. There has to be some *reason*, related to your product or service, the reader will look at your headline and say, "I'd better see what this is all about."

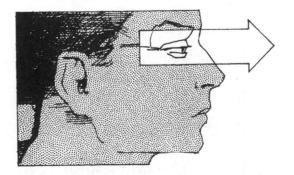

ASK DR. DIRECT . . .

"Several businesses similar to mine are already advertising in my local paper. How can I make my ad stand out from the rest?"

Here are some tips for writing standout headlines:

☞ *Keep it short, simple, and understandable.* It doesn't have to be overly clever, or funny, or complex. If your product is unusual, simply stating what it is may be enough. "Back-saving Backpacks" or "Men's Wide Shoes" are likely to draw in readers with those specific interests.

☞ *Include a benefit.* "Add More Fun Time to Your Vacation with Smith's Wrinkle-Resistant Travel Clothes" lets travelers know that buying from Smith's will give them more free time because they won't have to deal with steaming or ironing their clothes. If the biggest benefit for your customers is price, emphasize that. If your product does something specific, like help people lose 10 pounds in two weeks, that's what the headline should state.

☞ *Provoke the reader's curiosity.* Make an outrageous statement. (But make sure that it's true. No lies allowed.) "It Took 200 Years to Come Up with a Recipe Good Enough for Mrs. Collins' Crunchy Cobbler." Then your copy can go on to tell the story of how Mrs. Collins herself searched through her great-great-grandmother's diaries for the perfect cobbler recipe.

☞ *Solve a reader's problem.* If your product or service solves a common problem, readers will immediately identify with you. "Spend Too Much of Your Vacation Time Steaming (your clothes, that is)? Smith's Wrinkle-Resistant Travel Clothes Give You More Time to Enjoy Yourself." The problem can be posed as a question, and the answer can be included in the headline or contained in the ad copy.

☞ *Include a testimonial.* The testimonial can come from a celebrity ("Pro-Walkers Are the Most Comfortable Shoes I've Ever Worn Off the Court"—Pete Smith, U.S. Open Champion), or an authority in the field ("I Recommend Pro-Walkers for All My Patients"—Dr. Dean Hadley, Head of the Podiatry Society). Testimonials don't have to be from well-known names, however. This headline also works: "My Flat Feet Kept Me from Enjoying Long Walks for 20 Years. Six Months After Buying Pro-Walkers, I'm Walking Six Miles a Day"—Mrs. Cornelia Cooper, Rutland, Vermont. Even though I may not know Mrs. Cooper, my reaction is "If she can do it, I can do it too."

HEADLINE-WRITING WORKSHEET

Use this worksheet to practice writing headlines for your product or service. Try several different types until you find the one that both suits your company's "personality" and will be sure to grab readers' attention. Before you begin, list the features and benefits of your product. Try to include one or more benefits in every headline.

FEATURES   **BENEFITS**

_____   _____

_____   _____

_____   _____

Write a headline using a short, descriptive sentence about your product or service:

_____

_____

Write a headline that includes a benefit of your product or service:

_____

_____

Write a headline that provokes a reader's curiosity:

_____

_____

Write a headline that solves a reader's problem:

_____

_____

Write a headline that includes a testimonial:

_____

_____

THE BODY COPY

How long should your ad copy be? As long as it takes to get your message across. A four-line classified ad can be as effective as a full-page advertisement. A lot depends on your budget, of course. But no matter what the size of your ad, remember several things when creating body copy:

- *The copy should follow the lead of the headline.* If the headline asks a question, the answer should be found in the copy. If the headline has a humorous tone, the ad should too. If your headline makes statistical claims ("95% of people using our product grow hair in 30 days or less"), they should be substantiated in the copy.

- *Use fascinations.* Fascinations are short, punchy sentences that tell you exactly how you're going to benefit from using this product. ("No more counting calories! Never go hungry again! Enjoy your favorite foods!") Give people several good reasons they should buy from you and they probably will.

- *Include graphics.* If you have enough room, include an illustration or photograph of the product. Even better, enclose a picture of someone using the product. Even a small graphic can be an attention grabber and help your ad stand out.

- *Include a special offer.* If you are sending a direct mail letter, you might have two or three pages in which to entice buyers. Ad space is much more limited, but even the smallest ad should contain an incentive to buy, whether it's a discounted price ("10% off"), a multiple product offer ("Order two and get the second one for half price") or a free premium ("Order now and get our sturdy tote bag FREE!")

- *Keep the copy visually interesting.* Use crossheads as mini-headlines to keep readers interested. Utilize a variety of typefaces and type sizes (but don't overdo it).

THE OFFER

We'll discuss offers in depth in Part V. The offer is the special promotion or added incentive to help a prospect make the decision to buy—and buy now. There are many types of offers; whichever one you choose should be prominently featured in the copy of the ad.

THE ORDER FORM

All the rules that apply to order forms in the direct mail package apply to the direct response ad as well. The order form must be both large enough to be legible and large enough for people to fill in their information. It should reiterate your offer and make it as easy as possible for people to order from you. See pages 44–45 in Part III, "Creating a Direct Mail Package."

Not every direct response ad includes an order form. If your ad is three or four lines in the classified section or one square inch inside the magazine or newspaper, there may not be room for a full-fledged order form. There must be a way for people to order, however. You should include your 800 number (if you have one) or an address where people can send a check or money order. Make sure that it's a street address, not a post office box. People like to know exactly where they're sending the money.

DIRECT RESPONSE AD CHECKLIST

❏ Tantalize the reader with an interesting headline that grabs immediate attention.

❏ Use visual variety (e.g., crossheads, bold typeface, two colors, etc.) to keep people reading through.

❏ Include benefit statements that let the reader know why they should buy this product—from you—right now!

❏ Include a strong call to action ("Order before January 1, and take an additional 10% off the already low purchase price!").

❏ Make sure your ordering device is clearly legible and that you've given readers all the information they need to order from you. Always include your address, even if you have an 800 (or 888) number. An address reassures prospective customers, who may never have heard of your company, that you are a legitimate business.

❏ If possible, show your product in the ad. If you're selling a service, include testimonials from satisfied customers.

❏ Include a source code at the bottom of the ad. You can add it to the address, such as Dept. S, if you were running it in *Sunset* magazine. That way, if you place an ad in several different publications, you'll know which ones brought you the best results. If someone calls you to respond to the ad, be sure to ask where he or she heard about your product. Tracking your responses is the only way you can figure out the rate of response you got based on the circulation of that particular publication.

EXAMPLES: *Direct Response Ads*

Following are two successful direct response ads. Both were created by Westport, Connecticut, freelance writer and creative strategist Christopher England.

This two-inch-square ad ran in *Seventeen* magazine. The ad plays on the fact that teenage girls love gemstones and love to exchange friendship gifts. Although it is a small ad, it contains most of the elements we talked about for an effective ad:

Ad in *Seventeen* Magazine

✔ The headline is simple and straightforward: "Genuine Friendship Rubies." It is geared toward teenage girls, so it emphasizes friendship—something very important to that age range.

✔ The body copy tells prospective customers what the rubies will do for them: show their friend how much they care and melt their friend's heart.

✔ The product is pictured at its actual size.

✔ There are several calls to action that make it imperative to order now: "Don't miss out . . . They're selling like mad . . . Hurry and order . . . Your friendship depends on it!"

✔ The ordering device includes the offer of two free gift pouches and two free gift cards. It also includes the address for customers to send their money.

The following full-page ad was designed to be an free-standing insert in the Sunday edition of a national newspaper. It too includes all the elements of a successful direct response ad:

✔ **The headline** is clear and simple, and emphasizes the price value of "100 GIANT paper dolls for only 10¢ each!"

✔ The ad shows several of the dolls and makes sure the reader knows that they are really a full eight inches tall.

✔ **The body copy** has crossheads that keep the eye moving down the ad, toward the order form.

✔ The copy contains vivid imagery that puts the reader right inside the action: "Sit down with a cup of tea and warm cookies and remember the carefree times of childhood . . . ," and "Share quiet times with a daughter, granddaughter, or special young lady . . ."

✔ The bordered box announcing the dolls as a 1997 Award for Excellence winner from the Paper Doll Collectors Society of America gives the offer added credibility.

✔ **The offer** of a FREE personalized gift bag is emphasized several times in the body copy as well as just above the order form.

✔ **The order** form is large enough to be clearly legible, reiterates the fact that the dolls are only 10¢ apiece, and includes a "100% Guarantee of Satisfaction."

HOW TO EFFECTIVELY USE ADVERTISING SPACE

Now that you've designed the perfect ad for your product or service, where will it go? And how do you get advertising space once you've made your decision? The following steps describe what you need to know:

▶ *Review your target audience.* The first thing you need to do is go back to Part I, page 9, and review your target market to determine which newspapers or magazines your potential buyers might read. If you're selling something like the friendship rubies, which were aimed for girls aged 13–18, you might choose magazines like *Teen* and *Seventeen*. If your buyers are senior citizens, you might want to advertise in *Modern Maturity*. If you have a more general category of buyer, a regional or national magazine or newspaper might be best.

▶ *Decide which publications your buyers might read.* To find magazines and newspapers that fit the categories you have chosen, you can go to the library and look up *Standard Rate and Data* or *Bacon's Publicity Services.* Both publications will give you lists of magazines and newspapers (in separate volumes) divided into categories (such as automobiles, teens, seniors, womens, mens, sports, etc.). You can find out what each publication's advertising rates are, when various issues are coming out and, most important, the name and phone number of the advertising director.

▶ *Call the publisher for rates and a media kit.* You can then call the magazine directly and ask them to send you a media kit and a rate card. The media kit comes in handy if you're not familiar with the magazine. Examine the publication. Look at the kinds of ads it contains. Are they advertising the kinds of products your target audience might enjoy? Are there other direct response ads in the publication? If so, this is a good match for you. The kit will include a copy of their latest issue, along with some statistics about their readership and circulation. The kit will also include a rate card, which will tell you how much it costs to place various size ads (in color or black and white) in the publication. It will also give you discount prices for multiple placements (if you place three or four ads, you will get a discount).

HOW TO EFFECTIVELY USE ADVERTISING SPACE (continued)

▶ *Calculate your costs.* From there, you can figure out how much space you can afford and where you are getting the best deal. In a small-circulation magazine, you may be able to get a 1/3 page ad for $300. In a larger-circulation publication, it may cost you $3,000 for the same-size ad. Your goal is to get the largest space you can for the lowest cost per thousand (or CPM).

To determine the CPM, start with two numbers: the circulation and the cost of your ad. Suppose the circulation is 1,234,567 and the ad costs $9,000. Divide the circulation by 1,000, which is easy. Just drop the last three numbers so, for example, 1,234,567 becomes 1,234. Then divide the cost by that number to get the CPM.

$$\frac{\$9000}{1,234} = \$7.29$$

It will cost you $7.29 per 1,000 circulation.

WHAT TO EXPECT FROM YOUR AD

Don't expect to make a lot of money right away from direct response advertising. First of all, you have a lot of up-front costs the first time you place an ad. You'll have to pay for the design and production of the ad itself. When you place the ad again, you won't have those same up-front costs to consider.

Use these tips to get the most from your advertising dollar:

Use a media-buying service. You may be able to find such a service by checking the yellow pages or by calling your local chapter of the Direct Marketing Association. Media-buying services are agencies that buy volume space in various media and then sell that space to interested vendors. When an agency places an ad for you, they get a 15% professional discount.

Ask about remnant space. Many publications offer special rates for unsold space. That means that whenever the publication has an open space, they'll put your ad in. The good news is that you can usually get remnant space for a substantial discount. The bad news is that you never know exactly when your ad is going to run and you have to keep checking the publication to see if it has run.

TIP #3

Try an A-B split. This is a good way to test two different creative approaches or two different offers. In an A-B split, half the print run will contain one ad, and half will contain the other. The next time you place an ad, you can use the one that pulled the best response.

TIP #4

Ask for the right-hand page. Studies have proven that the right-hand page is read more often, and more carefully, than the left. The magazine may not guarantee you the right-hand page, but if you don't ask you'll probably end up on the left.

WHAT TO EXPECT FROM YOUR AD (continued)

 Use your direct response ad as a way to test your product. You may not get a resoundingly high response rate. But you can often attract customers who will buy from you for a long time. And it's a good way to test a particular strategy before you do a direct mail campaign.

When you fulfill your orders for direct response ads, include a *bounce-back offer*. A bounce-back is a promotion included in a shipment that offers the buyer a chance to buy another product from the same company. Oftentimes you don't make money from the ad, but you make money from the products purchased from bounce-back offers. You can offer the same product again (these buyers have a high propensity to buy again), or you can include a catalog of new products.

PART

V

The Offer

WHAT IS AN OFFER?

"I'm gonna make him an offer he can't refuse." Although offers in direct marketing don't have the same sinister connotations as that one, the concept is the same. You want to offer your prospective customers something so terrific, so irresistible, that they almost *have* to buy. Offers are the terms under which the product or service are sold.

Think about it. There you are, sitting at home, opening your mail. Or reading the daily newspaper. You're not out shopping, you're not looking for anything in particular. You open a direct mail package or turn the page of the newspaper. And there it is—a product you have never seen or considered buying before. What would make you get up out of your chair and pick up a pen to fill in the order form or pick up the phone and make a purchase?

Offers represent 40% of the success of your direct marketing campaign (the list represents 40% and the creative input represents 20%). Yet many marketers still send mail or create an ad that doesn't contain an offer—or they make the same offer that is available at retail stores. Your direct marketing offer should be unique, not available anywhere else. Your offer must be:

► **APPEALING.** You can make many different kinds of offers (see following page). A simple offer of 10% off can be effective, but it's also the same kind of offer everyone else is making. Your objective is to get prospective buyers to picture themselves already using your product or service—and feeling great because they *saved money* doing it, or *got something else along with it for little or no cost.* Consumers like to consider themselves savvy shoppers. Your offer should give them opportunity to feel that way.

► **BELIEVABLE.** If you offer a free gift that is worth thousands of dollars, consumers will be understandably skeptical. You want prospective customers to consider your offer to be a great deal—not something that is too good to be true.

► **CREATIVE.** The idea is to create a great offer, an unusual offer—something we call a "unique selling proposition." Your exercise video may be similar to many others on the market. But if your offer includes a FREE set of wrist and ankle weights to use while watching your video, customers may choose yours over the others. Study the offers you see in direct mail packages you receive and in the ads you read. Make notes about which ones appeal to you. And ask a group of people who fit into your target market which ones would appeal to them most.

OFFER CATEGORIES

There are several different categories of offers you can make. Feel free to mix and match to find the offer(s) that best suit your product or service.

► THE PRICE/DISCOUNT OFFER

This is the most commonly used offer, and it appears in many different forms. It can be presented as a dollar amount or a percentage discount. There are several ways to present your offer:

$10 off

20% off

A $50.00 value, now only $39.95

Because these kinds of offers are so commonly used, try to make them a little different. You might want to try an unexpected number, such as the following:

$12.01 off

44% off

A $50.00 value, now only $39.46

A price discount can also be very effective as a call to action:

Order before September 29 and take an extra 10% off the low purchase price. Remember, the special sale price of $39.46 goes back up to $50.00 after midnight on December 31!

► THE MULTIPLE-DISCOUNT OFFER

If you're offering a product and customers want to order more than one, they also want to be rewarded for their extra spending. There are many ways to reward these customers:

Buy One, Get the Second at Half-Price

Buy Two, Get One Free

Sale Price Only $8.99. Buy Two or More for Only $7.00 Each.

Service providers can also use multiple discounts by "bundling" offers:

Relax with our deep muscle massage, only $60 for one hour. Or pamper your face with a special cleansing facial for only $50. Better yet, get a massage and facial together for only $99.99!

Learn to speak Spanish! One-hour classes $19.95 each. Ten classes for only $179.95!

► **PREMIUMS**

A premium is an item that is offered free (or for a nominal price, or for the cost of shipping and handling) with the purchase of your product or service. A premium may be given to everyone who buys:

FREE GIFT with every order!

or only to customers who reach a certain spending level:

FREE faux-pearl necklace-and-earring set with every order of $50 or more.

A premium offer works best when it is somehow related to the product or service you're selling. An offer of a faux-pearl necklace may raise response rates for a clothing catalog, but it probably won't help sales of computer equipment. If you were selling computer equipment, an effective premium might be a personalized mousepad or a tiny calculator in the shape of a briefcase.

If you are considering offering a premium, keep the cost in mind. You want to find a premium that will lift response and pay for itself. If each product sale brings you a profit of $6, offering a premium that costs you $12 doesn't make sense. If your premium costs you $2, but increases your sales by 20%, you have increased your overall profit.

Where can you find premiums to offer? Premium and incentive trade shows are held in major cities at least once a year. You can also look in the yellow pages for companies that sell premium and incentive items. And you can check out direct marketing publications such as *Potentials in Marketing* (Minneapolis) and *DM News* (New York City).

OFFER CATEGORIES (continued)

► LOYALTY PROGRAMS

A loyalty program is anything you do to create an ongoing relationship with your customer. The most obvious example is the frequent-flyer program, in which airlines offer customers free miles for every mile they fly. A flyer who has 49,500 frequent-flyer miles on XYZ Airlines is going to be sure to fly another 500 miles with them in order to take advantage of their 50,000-mile bonus flight. The more miles the traveler collects, the better the bonus. This keeps XYZ Airlines and the frequent flyer "married" to each other.

You don't have to be a large airline in order to institute a loyalty program. There is a children's bookstore near my house that has a "baker's dozen" plan. Each time I buy something there, I tell them that I am on the plan. My purchase is recorded in the computer. After I buy my 12th item, I get number 13 for free. Now whenever I need a gift for a young child, the first place I think of going to is this bookstore. There are other book-stores I could shop at that are less expensive. But because this store is right in my neighborhood and I have already made six purchases, I will keep buying from them, and they will keep me as a loyal customer.

You can implement this type of program by offering bonus points, using a punch card, or giving rebates or dividends at the end of the year.

► CUSTOMER-RETENTION PROGRAMS

You don't have to give anything away to keep your customers coming back. You can use ongoing communications with your customers to build a loyal clientele. You can give them information, thank them for making a purchase, or send a holiday greeting. Here are some examples of customer-retention communications programs:

Fliers	*Holiday greetings*
Newsletters	*Thank-you notes*
Educational materials	*Personalized letters*
Birthday cards	

► EARLY-BIRD OFFERS

An early-bird offer is actually a call to action. It gets people to act immediately. If they take too much time to think about the offer, they'll ignore it. This means that you offer a special low price for a limited time only. Some early-bird offers might be:

Order before January 1, and get our special end-of-the-year rate.

If you register before June 15, the seminar fee is $199.99. After that date, the fee is $250.00.

The first 500 people to order the Acme Bread Baker will receive The Acme Bread-Baker Recipe Booklet *ABSOLUTELY FREE!*

► FREE SHIPPING AND HANDLING

For some reason, people often resent having to pay for shipping and handling. Even though realistically it may be a reasonable amount, it always seems like you're paying too much for this service. So when the shipping-and-handling charges are removed, the tendency to buy increases. It's hard to resist an offer like the following:

Buy Any Two of Dotty's Dolls and We Will Pay for Shipping. Buy Three or More and We'll Even Send It Overnight Express!

So as long as it doesn't cut into your profits, you might want to try paying for the shipping and handling yourself.

► MEMBER GET A MEMBER

Some of your best customers are going to be those who have been referred to you by people who currently buy from you. If they've heard about you through a friend or family member, they already have a good impression of your company and your product or service. You want to encourage your customers to refer others to you, and reward them when they do. MCI became famous for this with their Friends and Family service. As a customer, you get a discount for referring other customers, and a lower rate when you call someone else who also uses MCI.

Your reward system can be given as points, in which the customer earns so many bonus points for each person he or she refers. You can give a free gift or a straightforward discount, with a dollar amount or percentage off. For instance:

Do Your Friends a Favor! Refer a Friend or Relative to Dr. Smith's Chiropractic and Get Your Next Visit Free!

Get a Friend to Sign Up with Ace Cellular Phone and Take 50% Off Next Month's Bill!

OFFER CATEGORIES (continued)

▶ **DELUXE EDITIONS**

With this type of offer, you present your product in two different versions. For instance, you might offer a limited-edition lithograph of a beautiful landscape for $69.95. In the same ad or direct mail piece, you could also offer a framed version of the same lithograph for $99.95. Or, if you're offering a hardcover edition of a book for $29.95, you might also offer a leather-bound volume of the same book for $49.95. Once a customer has made the decision to buy your product, it's only a short leap to get them to buy the more expensive version.

▶ **PAYMENT OPTIONS**

The easier you make it for customers to buy from you, the greater the chances they will. The more choices you offer for how they can pay for your product or service, the easier you make it to buy. Simply giving the customers the choice of paying by check or by credit card increases your sales potential.

One popular payment option is the installment plan. When the home-shopping networks on television began offering "easy pay" plans, in which customers could pay for items in two or three installments, their sales increased significantly. If customers are considering a purchase of $100.00, you can make it easier for them by offering it in "three easy payments of $33.33." Some catalogs and direct response ads (especially those for collectible plates and dolls) don't even state the full price of the item. For instance, an ad may read:

> *For a Limited Time Only—the Incredibly Lifelike Portrait of Elvis at Graceland on a 12" Porcelain Plate. Yours for Only Three Easy Payments of $18.95, Plus Shipping and Handling.*

Other types of payment options include:

> *No money down*
> *No interest payments until . . .*
> *Order now, pay later*

► EXCLUSIVITY

Everyone wants to feel special, and everyone likes to feel that they have been specially chosen to belong to a particular group. If you have targeted your potential customers, you know that they have a special interest in what you offer. If you are selling golf equipment and accessories, then you want to address your prospects as golf lovers:

> *This is a special offer for those people who know the value of a good game of golf.*

Another offer of this kind is to invite people to join an exclusive club:

> *We know that you love a good game of golf. So do we. That's why we have traveled around the world, looking for the very best courses—and the accommodations that surround them. We are inviting you and a small group of others to become charter members of the Great Golf Getaways Club. Every six weeks, we will send you our exclusive catalog, which includes unbelievable prices on golf vacation packages, equipment, clothing, and shoes. We look forward to having you as a member.*

► FREE TRIALS

In most cases, once customers get an item into their homes, they won't return it. Offering a free trial allows customers the option to buy, and then to send it back if they don't like it. Chances are they will like it. Even if they don't, chances are they'll keep it anyway. The Direct Marketing Association reports that less than 5% of items ordered are returned (although this figure is higher for clothing items). So even if we're not sure whether or not we really like what we've ordered, it's usually easier to keep it than to take the time and effort to repack it and return it. But people want to know that they have the option to try out the merchandise and return it if they want to.

A free trial is another way of saying "Money-Back Guarantee." This is something that should be included in every direct marketing campaign. People need to be reassured that if they have somehow made a mistake in ordering, they can get their money back.

If you are selling a more complex item, like exercise equipment or electronics, you might want to include a warranty, which spells out exactly what repairs and returns your company is responsible for. In that case, you must follow certain rules and regulations laid out by the Federal Trade Commission. To find out more about guarantees and warranties, you can send away for the FTC booklet, *Businessperson's Guide to Federal Warranty Law,* Federal Trade Commission, 6th Street & Pennsylvania Avenue NW, Washington, DC 20580.

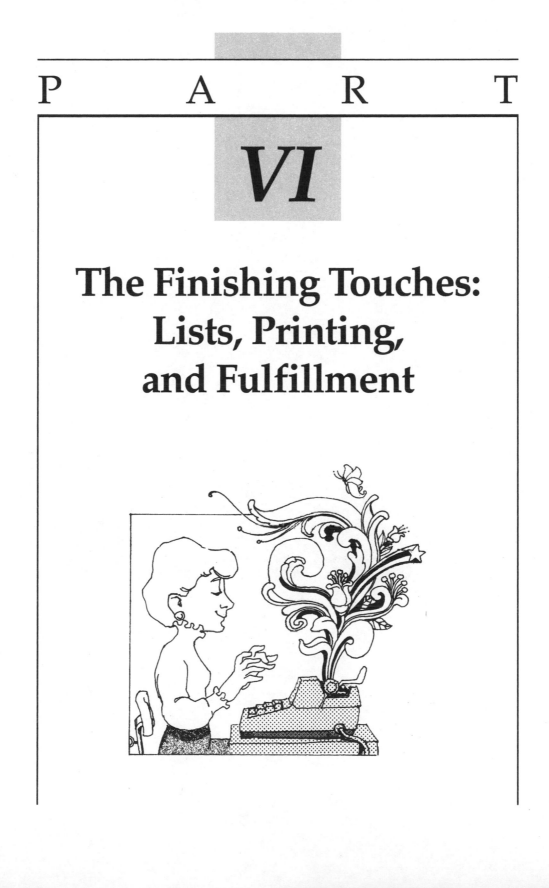

PART

VI

The Finishing Touches:
Lists, Printing,
and Fulfillment

MAILING LISTS

Suppose you put together a terrific direct mail package, beautifully written and designed, for Talking Turtles, stuffed toys containing computer chips that allow kids to tape-record and play back their own voices. You've included an irresistible offer. Should be pretty easy to sell, right? Not necessarily. A lot depends on your ability to get this direct mail package into the right hands. If you send the package off to a group of financial advisors, for instance, you probably won't get much of a response. There's no relationship between financial advisors and kids' toys. Some advisors may have children, but it would be a hit-or-miss effort. If you just send the mailing out to a random group of names, you won't get much response either. You have no way of knowing how many of those random names might be interested in kids' toys.

> **Forty% of the success of your campaign depends on marketing to the right mailing list; therefore, choosing the best possible list is of great importance.**

A mailing list is made up of names and addresses of individuals who share some common characteristics. Those characteristics might include geographic location, activities, hobbies, age, sex, or income level. There are three basic types of mailing lists:

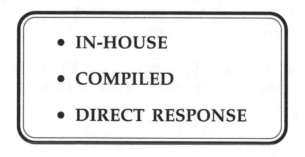

- **IN-HOUSE**

- **COMPILED**

- **DIRECT RESPONSE**

MAILING LISTS (continued)

The In-House List

This list, also called a *house file*, comprises your own customers, as well as prospects who have inquired about your products or services. These people are highly likely to buy from you. If your business is fairly small or you are just starting out, this may be the only list you use. Your customers are your greatest asset, so keeping this list carefully maintained is of great importance. And your list should be constructed so that you can pull out pertinent information when you need it—information that will tell you who your best customers are, which is usually determined by three factors: recency, frequency, and monetary.

- ▶ **Recency** tells you when this customer last ordered from you. Was it a year ago? Six months ago? Last month? The more recently the customer made a purchase, the more likely he or she will purchase again.

- ▶ **Frequency** tells you how many times this customer has ordered from you.

- ▶ **Monetary** refers to the average amount of an order from that customer. If the customer has made three purchases during the last year, one for $50, one for $125, and one for $65, then the average amount of her order would be $80.

Keeping track of your customers' RFM ratings will let you know exactly who your top buyers are. These are your best customers, and they should be rated as such.

The Compiled List

A compiled list is made up of names and addresses of people who have one basic characteristic in common. The characteristic might be occupation; association membership; purchasers of a particular make or brand of a specific product (such as people who've bought Ford Explorers); people who live in a particular geographic location, etc. Compiled lists are derived from telephone books, public records, business and association directories, and car and voter registrations. Examples of compiled lists might be all chiropractors in the state of Michigan; all members of the Direct Marketing Association; all people living in zip code 10025; or all families with children attending elementary school in Chicago.

Compiled lists are often used by business-to-business marketers. If you were selling a product for chiropractors, for instance, you might be interested in the list of all chiropractors in the state of Michigan. Compiled lists are usually less expensive than direct response lists—and less effective. That's because there's no way of telling whether the people on these lists have ever responded to direct marketing offers—and those are the people you're trying to reach.

The Direct Response List

A direct response list consists of the names and addresses of people who have previously purchased products or services from a company other than your own. In other words, they have at some time bought something through the mail, either from a direct mail solicitation or from direct response advertising. Studies have shown that once people have purchased something via direct marketing, they are very likely to make such a purchase again.

HOW TO CHOOSE A LIST

Once again, it's time to go back and review your description of your ideal customers. What characteristics do they have in common? Are they predominately one gender? What is their age range? Do they have similar interests or hobbies in common? What is their income level? The more you know about your own customers, the easier it will be to find lists that match their profiles.

Using a List Broker

With more than 15,000 lists available in the United States, finding the ones appropriate for your business would be almost impossible to achieve on your own. Luckily for all direct marketers, there are list brokers who match up direct marketers with list owners. There is no cost to you for their services (they get a commission from the list owners), and they can provide you with valuable suggestions and information.

You can find a list broker by calling your local chapter of the Direct Marketing Association, or by looking in the *Direct Marketing Market Place* (also known as the *DMMP*). If you can't find this book in your local library, you can order a copy by calling (301) 604-0187. This directory contains list brokers (and many more direct marketing service providers) nationwide.

You might want to call two or three list brokers and get suggestions from all of them. You may want to go with one who has done some "creative" list planning. If you use only the obvious choices—companies that have a direct relationship to your product or service—remember that these lists will also be chosen by everyone else selling products similar to yours. If possible, you want to look for people who have not already received product offers similar to yours. That means you need a creative list broker who can come up with new ideas to find your best prospects.

Get Creative

There is one directory you should consult yourself, the *Standard Rate and Data Service List Directory*. Most lists on the market are listed here and you'll probably get some ideas of your own when you review it. Then pass those suggestions on to your list broker, who may have some insights about how that list will perform for your product and offer.

Tips for Using a List Broker

▶ **Ask the broker for client references you can call.** You want to know if the lists the broker suggested to these clients performed well. If the clients were dissatisfied with the results, call another broker.

▶ **Describe your goals, direct mail package, and target market to the list broker.** Tell her what it is you're selling and who you're trying to reach. The list broker will make recommendations based on the information you supply.

▶ **Ask the broker to design a list plan for you.** After you've described your goals and criteria to the broker, he will put together a plan for you with suggestions of lists he thinks will work for your product or service. An experienced list broker, with knowledge of the thousands of lists available and which lists have worked well for companies similar to yours, can be invaluable in helping you reach your target prospects.

▶ **Once you choose the lists you want, ask the broker who has used the list in the past.** If the list has been successful for a product or service similar to yours, it will probably be successful for you as well. However, you might not want to use a list if your direct competitor has used it recently. The list broker can tell you just who has used the list, and how well it performed for them.

Once you've spoken to the broker and asked him to design a list for you, he'll send you a list card for each company he recommends. The following is a typical list card (this one is for a fictional company called The Collector's Corner), and an explanation of the information you'll find there.

List Card

The Collector's Corner

09/99

7

1
143,412 1998–1999 Buyers $80.00M
62,335 Last 12 months Buyers + $10.00M
38,166 Last 6 months Hotline + $10.00M
Buyers

8
AVG unit of
sale: $45.00

2
Description of buyers:
Direct response purchasers of collectible items
such as miniature teapots, resin figurines,
ceramic masks, etc.
Respondents have an average income of
$40,000
Average age is 50+

9
Sex:
73% Female
27% Male
(selectable)

10
Addressing:
4-up Cheshire
P/S Labels $5.00
9T 1600/6250 BPI
$25.00 Flat Fee
Nonrefundable

3
Restrictions:
No direct competition; no contests or
sweepstakes; no telemarketing

11
Key Coding:
$2.00M

4
Source:
Direct mail and space ads

12
Minimum order:
5,000

5
Selections:
State, Zip Code, Sex $5.00M
Hotline Buyers $10.00M

13
Net Name:
85% + $5.00M
Running charge
50,000 minimum

6
Notes:
1) Cancellation of order after mail date will
require payment in full.
2) Cancellation prior to mail date will require
a $75.00 flat fee.

14
*Update
Schedule:*
Bi-Annually

15
Requirements:
Sample Mailing

Components of a List Card

1. **Number of Buyers and Cost Per Thousand:** This tells you how many names are on this list, as well as how many people bought in the last year (or last quarter, or last month). It also tells you how much it costs, per thousand names, to rent this list. Costs typically run from $75 to $125 per 1,000 names. Hotline buyers are the ones who have bought most recently.

2. **Description of Buyers:** This is a general description of the product or service the company sells, and a short description of their typical customers.

3. **Restrictions:** Companies can make their own rules as to who can and cannot rent their lists. Companies rarely rent to their direct competitors. Some companies don't want their customers contacted by telemarketers or inundated with contests or sweepstakes. When you rent a list, it is for a one-time use only: you can't use the list over and over again. Companies always include "decoy" names on the list to check that only one mailing was sent.

4. **Source:** Where did the company get the names it is willing to rent to you? In this case, The Collector's Corner got the names from people who purchased directly from their catalog or ordered from direct response advertising in a newspaper or magazine (also called a *space ad*).

5. **Selections:** You want to narrow down your mailing list as much as possible so that it best matches your target market. If 90% of your customers are women, you may want to mail only to women from the Collector's Corner list. Or, if you want to mail only to a specific geographic area, you can select only certain states or zip codes. This section tells you what selections are available from this list. You pay an additional fee for each selection you choose.

6. **Notes:** These are the company's rules about canceling your order. When you rent a list, you must tell the company when you plan to do your mailing. If you decide to cancel your mailing before the planned date, you must pay a cancellation fee. If you decide to cancel your mailing after the planned date, you must pay the full amount.

7. **Date:** This is the date that this list was compiled. You want the most recently compiled list you can get.

Components of a List Card (continued)

8. **Average Unit of Sale:** This tells you how much the typical Collector's Corner customer spends on an order. When choosing a mailing list, you want to find prospects who can afford your products, so you want to choose a unit of sale equal to or higher than your own.

9. **Sex:** This is a breakdown of the company's customers according to sex. If your company sells mostly to men, and this company sells mainly to women, you may want to choose another list.

10. **Addressing:** There are several ways you can address your envelopes or catalogs. You can use Cheshire labels, which are printed out on computer paper and glued onto mailing envelopes. P/S stands for pressure-sensitive labels, which are self-adhesive and can be removed from the envelope or catalog and attached to an order blank or card. "9T 1600/6250 BPI" represents the format used for a list stored on magnetic tape. If you're going to send personalized letters, you must use magnetic tape. Talk to your lettershop to find out which format is best for you to use.

11. **Key Coding:** If you want to know which orders came from the Collector's Corner list, you must add a key code to each label. That will cost you an additional $2 per 1,000 names.

12. **Minimum Order:** Most direct response lists have a 5,000-name minimum.

13. **Net Name:** This is a discount arrangement for large-volume orders (usually 50,000 or more). If you rent several lists from several different companies, there are bound to be duplicates. You would then use a process called *merge/purge* to eliminate the duplications. Net names allows you to pay only for the names you use (with a minimum of 85%), plus a running charge.

14. **Update Schedule:** Just how hot are the hotline buyers on this list? This tells you how often the list is updated. So if you were looking for lists in May, and you know that Collector's Corner updates its lists in June, you might want to wait the extra month to rent the list.

15. **Requirements:** Most companies will ask to see a sample of your mailing piece before they will rent you their list. If you don't have a finished version printed yet, you can send them a simulated version that includes the written copy and an artist's rendering of any graphics you plan to include.

COMPUTER SERVICE BUREAUS

When your own in-house mailing list gets large enough, or when you rent lists of several thousand names and start doing major mailings, you'll probably want to use a lettershop and a computer service bureau. A lettershop is a company with the machinery necessary for inserting, addressing, applying postage to, and sorting mail for delivery to the post office. The stop between the printer and the lettershop is the computer service bureau. These are companies that build and maintain databases. Computer service bureaus perform four main functions:

1. LIST MAINTENANCE

When you rent lists from several different companies, they may all be in different formats. The first thing the service bureau will do is standardize the lists so that they can all be merged into one large database of your customers or prospects.

2. LIST PREPARATION

As I mentioned earlier, if you rent lists from different companies, there are bound to be duplications. John Doe of One Main Street, Anytown, USA, may appear on several of the lists, but you don't want to send him duplicate mailings. So the service bureau performs a merge/purge operation, which eliminates the duplicates. This is done in a democratic fashion so that all the names are not taken off one list.

3. VALIDATING ADDRESS INFORMATION

The service bureau will run your lists through software developed by the post office called the *Certified Accuracy Support System*, which validates that the names on the list are being sent to deliverable addresses.

4. POSTAL SORTATION

The post office requires that large mailings be sorted into various categories, such as nine-digit zip codes and carrier routes. The more categories into which you sort your mail, the bigger the discount you get on your mailing costs.

PRINTING

Printing is one of the facets of direct marketing that can most influence your profit margin. You may have an idea for a fantastic four-color brochure with cutouts and stickers, but the cost may make it almost impossible for you to break even on your campaign.

That's why you should always get printing estimates before you begin designing the direct mail package. Make rough drafts of your ideas (with all the bells and whistles) and bring them to several printers. Get estimates for printing costs. Be as specific as you can about each piece you intend to have printed. You'll need to give the printer information about six different factors:

1. **SIZE:** If you want your letter or brochure printed in an odd size, it may cost more because it won't fit any standard press sizes. However, you may be able to take advantage of *ganging*, printing more than one piece on the same press at the same time. For instance, if your odd-size letter leaves room on one side, you may be able to print an order form or coupon in the leftover space.

2. **PAPER STOCK:** The type of paper you choose can make a big difference in your printing cost. Paper comes in two finishes: coated and uncoated. Letters, books, and anything featuring a lot of text are usually printed on uncoated stock. Brochures, catalogs, magazines, and anything that contains reprints of photographs are usually printed on coated stock. If you want to print on coated or colored paper, that will add to your costs.

3. **PAPER WEIGHT:** Because postage costs are determined by weight, the total weight of your printed package can make a difference. But you don't want to print on anything too flimsy, or it will create a bad impression on your customers.

4. **INK COLOR:** It's not the particular color that increases costs, it's the number of colors you use. The more colors you want to add, the greater the cost.

5 **TIME:** This is where many direct marketers get into trouble. They don't leave enough time for the printing to be done, and therefore incur extra rush charges. Be sure to plan far enough in advance so that the printer has plenty of time for your job.

6 **SIZE OF RUN:** One reason you need to shop around for printers is that some are equipped to handle small jobs and others are equipped for larger runs. Small runs are usually printed on a sheet-fed press, which rolls individual sheets of paper through each color press. Larger runs are printed on a web press, which runs huge continuous rolls of paper through the presses. Not every printer has both types of equipment, so be sure to let the printer know how many pieces you want to mail.

PRINTING ESTIMATE SPECIFICATION SHEET

Remember that price isn't everything. A printer who gives you the lowest price may not produce the highest quality. Be sure to ask to see samples of other direct mail pieces, and ask for client references.

Fill in your specifications and give to the printer for estimates.

SIZE OF PIECES:

❑ LETTER _____

❑ LIFT LETTER _____

❑ ORDER FORM _____

❑ BROCHURE _____

❑ OUTER ENVELOPE _____

❑ BUSINESS REPLY ENVELOPE OR CARD _____

PAPER STOCK:

❑ COATED

❑ UNCOATED

INK COLOR:

❑ ONE

❑ TWO

❑ THREE

❑ FOUR

DATE NEEDED: _____

SIZE OF THE RUN (NUMBER OF PIECES): _____

FULFILLMENT

Customers have great expectations when they order through the mail or over the telephone. They've read a description of your product or seen a photograph in a catalog. They expect to receive that product, just the way it has been described, in a timely fashion. If you do not meet those expectations, you are headed for failure.

Fulfillment includes all the activities that go on once a customer's order is received: opening or taking orders, entering the order information in a computer, preparing a label and/or invoice, selecting the correct merchandise to fill the order, and shipping the merchandise to the customer. It can also include customer service and taking care of returns.

You have three options when it comes to fulfillment. You can:

- Handle both the order taking and the shipping in-house

- Take the orders in-house and have an outside service handle the shipping

- Have an outside service handle both the order taking and shipping

How do you know which option is best for you? There are three main factors to consider:

▶ *How large is your company?* If your organization is very small and you're running on a tight budget, you might want to handle everything yourself. You can always go to outside services as your business grows.

▶ *What is the size of your staff?* Do you have the personnel available to handle order taking and shipping merchandise? If you have to hire and train new people to handle these functions, you should weigh these costs against hiring outside services.

▶ *How large is your facility?* Do you have enough room to store your goods? Many people run their businesses out of a spare room or garage. But if your products are large or you're selling a catalog's worth of various merchandise, you may not have the space to keep your products stored properly.

HANDLING THE ORDERS

Direct marketers are often so anxious to get their mailings out they don't take the time to consider what will happen when the orders come rolling in. You must be prepared and have everything in place long before you take the first order; otherwise, you're likely to lose many customers. Whether you're handling the process yourself or an outside service is doing it for you, the same essentials must be in place, including:

▶ **MAILING ADDRESS:** Where are customers going to send their orders? Do you want thousands of people sending mail to your home address? You can use a post office box, but it's a good idea to include a street address as well. People are leery of businesses with only a post office box return address; they want reassurance that the business (especially if they've never heard of you before) really exists.

▶ **TELEPHONE NUMBER:** A survey by the Direct Marketing Association has shown that more than two-thirds of people questioned chose calling a toll-free number as their first option for ordering merchandise. Are you going to make a toll-free number available to your customers? If so, will you have people available to answer calls 24 hours a day? This is especially important if you're sending mailings across several different time zones.

If you choose not to install your own 800 (or 888) number, there are telemarketing services you can use. You'll need to work closely with the telephone service representatives to develop a script that they will follow without sounding like robots. Remember that customers won't know they're dealing with telemarketers—they'll assume they're speaking directly with your company. So you need to be satisfied that they are friendly and treat your customers with the same courtesy and respect as you would.

▶ **PAYMENT OPTIONS:** How will your customers pay for their merchandise? Cash? Checks? Credit cards? Most direct marketers do not offer the option of paying in cash. It's just too easy for cash to get lost somewhere along the line. That leaves checks and credit cards. If you want to offer credit card options, you must set up accounts with a bank (for MasterCard or Visa) or with the credit card company (for American Express or Discover). It can be difficult to establish such accounts; both banks and credit card companies are often reluctant to set up accounts with start-up mail order businesses.

If you can't get your own account, there are credit card processing services that will handle these transactions for you (for a fee, of course). Accepting credit card orders can substantially increase your sales; therefore, you should weigh the costs of the service against the additional dollars you receive.

► **ORDER ENTRY:** If you are handling the orders yourself, you must have a way to keep track of your customers and the merchandise they ordered. There are many different computer programs you can use. Some can be bought off the shelf. Check publications such as *Direct Marketing* magazine, *DM News,* and *Home Office Computing* for their reviews and recommendations. Ask other small businesses in your area what programs they use. Or you can have a computer programmer design a program to fit your special needs. But be sure your program allows you to input such information as:

- Customer name
- Address
- Phone number
- Date of order
- Method of payment

- Items ordered
- Dollar amount received
- Shipping & handling payments received
- Sales tax received
- Source code

Your program should also include some method of inventory control. You need to know how many of each item you have in stock and how many are backordered (temporarily out of stock).

ASK DR. DIRECT . . .

"I've decided to use an outside fulfillment service. How do I know if they're doing a good job?"

The best way to tell if they're doing a good job is to become a customer of your own company:

☞ *Call the toll-free number and place an order (using another name), or get a friend to do it.* Were the operators friendly? Courteous? Could they answer your questions?

☞ *Order the same items by mailing in an order form.* Pay by check. Add the total incorrectly and see how the mistake is handled. Pay by credit card and then return the item. Do you get a refund in a timely fashion?

☞ *Check the package once it arrives.* Did it come to you in good condition? Was the packaging pleasing and attractive? Was it delivered to you on time? Was everything you ordered in the package? If not, were you given notification of when the remaining items would be shipped?

SHIPPING RULES AND REGULATIONS

The government has established rules that must be followed where mail order is concerned. The first is the *Mail-Order Rule*, established over 20 years ago, which states that a company must ship merchandise within the amount of time indicated in a catalog or an advertisement, or within 30 days if no time is indicated. If you cannot ship an item within 30 days, you are required to notify the customer and give them the option of requesting a refund. If the customer requests a refund, or if you are not able to fulfill the order for any reason, you must refund the correct amount by first-class mail within seven working days after the order is canceled. If the customer paid by credit card, you must credit the customer's account within one billing cycle.

Here is typical letter you can use to inform customers of backordered merchandise:

Talking Turtles Toys
14 Buena Vista Boulevard
Van Nuys, CA 90045

Ms. Cathy Customer
101 North Elm Street
Anytown, USA 10010

Dear Ms. Customer,

Thank you for your recent order. Unfortunately, because of [*fill in reason for the delay*] we are not able to ship your order for [*fill in item description*] at this time.

We expect to ship this item to you on or before [*fill in ship date*]. If we do not hear from you before then, we will ship the item to you. If you wish to cancel your order or replace it with a substitute item, please return the enclosed postage-paid reply card.

We appreciate having you as a Talking Turtles Toys customer and apologize for any inconvenience.

Sincerely,

Name
Title

SHIPPING RULES AND REGULATIONS (continued)

There are other rules and regulations that have been set up by the Federal Trade Commission (FTC). These rules involve regulations against making false claims about your product. You can't claim that your product performs miracles unless you have proof that this is true. You can't make false claims about prices; you can't state that an item now on sale for $14.95 formerly sold at $69.95 unless a substantial number were sold at that price. And you are responsible for any claims made in testimonials for your product. If you use a testimonial by Cathy Customer about the miracles performed by your product, and her statements are false, you can still be charged with false advertising even if you didn't know she was lying.

You cannot sell the following categories of items through the mail:

- Pornographic and obscene materials

- New drugs (you must get special permission from the Food and Drug Administration)

- Lotteries

- Pyramid or chain schemes

If you would like more information on the mail-order rule or any other FTC regulations regarding mail order, you can call (202) 326-3175 or write to them at:

> Division of Enforcement
> Federal Trade Commission
> 6th Street & Pennsylvania Avenue NW
> Washington, DC 20580

P A R T

VII

Ask Dr. Direct: Most Frequently Asked Questions

Dear Dr. Direct:

I'm interested in the potential of direct marketing as a profitable business venture. How do I find a product to sell?

You're probably doing it backwards. The best way to start is with an idea for a product (or service) and then find a way to sell it; and if direct marketing is the best way, great. DM works best when you believe in what you're selling, when you're enthusiastic, expert, customer oriented, etc. That's hard to do when you're just going to be selling any old product. So sit down and think about it. What makes you enthusiastic? What do you know a lot about? How can you relate to the people who might buy it? Then get excited about DM as a profitable business venture. As they said years ago in a book . . . do what you love and the money will follow.

Failing that, do some homework. See what sells in magazines with a lot of space ads. Try the *New Yorker, Yankee, National Enquirer,* airlines' in-flight magazines, etc., and see what sells in them. Make a list and then pick something that appeals to you. That might work.

∽

Dear Dr. Direct:

I've just opened an exercise club here in Springfield. We're mailing to fitness-magazine subscribers, and I wonder if I should try advertising on radio and TV. If I do, should all the efforts have a unified theme?

Maybe not a theme but certainly a look and voice. Get a strong logo. Make lots of cool offers. Try a guarantee, free intro sessions, etc. You might want to consider talking about your state-of-the-art equipment, personal trainers, etc. Socializing is a big part of the fitness game so mention that, too. Couch everything in terms of benefits, and make it easy to respond and track response. Look for sales spikes shortly after your commercials.

∽

Dear Dr. Direct:

We're about to send our first catalog. We're a start-up and nobody's ever heard of us. I know that people hesitate buying if a company doesn't have an established reputation. What can we do to overcome this?

Let's see . . . you could partner with an established company . . . or develop a PR campaign to get some press before you launch . . . or do the catalog in such a professional and confident way that people who see it will think you've been in the business for ages and they've just never heard of you until now. Or hire a celebrity to be your spokesperson or even your model . . . or use a lot of testimonial-type quotes from established businesses . . . or be so upbeat, so confident, so expert sounding, so likable, so full of personality, that you'll be irresistible. The doctor would be happier, though, if you started with small space ads in direct response magazines. You'd find out which products sell best, get a feel for the market and response management, start building a database of customers, generate some cash . . . and by the time you mail your catalog, more people will have heard of you.

Dear Dr. Direct:

Do I have to send my direct mail pieces first class? Do customers respond as well to third-class mail?

1) No. 2) It's close.

The difference between first and third class ranges from about a dime to over 17¢, depending on how many pieces you're mailing and how much of the post office's work you do for them. Let's say you get an average 1.5% response with a third-class mailing and your profit per order is $25. With first class you'd be spending from $100 to $170 per 1,000 more for postage. To get that back you need four to seven more orders per 1,000 pieces mailed, which means your response rate would have to be 1.9% to 2.2%, a lift of more than 25% over your 1.5% response rate with third-class postable. Unlikely.

First or third class probably doesn't matter if the package is written and designed to be intriguing and attractive. People will look at your headline and graphics before they'll look at how much postage you've paid.

If you're going to send out a plain envelope and you insist on going first class, use a live stamp. And two stamps are better than one.

Dear Dr. Direct:

If we start a special program for our best customers, with special discounts, and maybe during presale shopping days, will it annoy our other customers if they find out?

Your "other" customers will resent it if they can't join the special program. You might try throwing your special program wide open by treating all your customers as special . . . if they buy something from you. There are a lot of different models to study. The Book of the Month Club does it in a neat way with bonus points; buy enough books to earn enough points and you get a FREE book. Around Christmas they give you a freebie if you buy $X worth of merchandise. It's a benefit available only to the best customers by definition, but anybody can qualify as a best customer. Everybody knows about it, and there's no resentment at all.

Or you could keep your best customer program a secret if you mail it only to your best customers. That's one of the great things about the mail; it's personal and one-to-one. If, by chance, a few people find out about it and complain, apologize and make them the same offer.

⹂

Dear Dr. Direct:

I get letters all the time with the salutation "Dear Friend," and it's beginning to bug me. There's got to be a better way to start a nonpersonalized letter.

The Dr. hears you . . .

Before you write the salutation, write the letter. Maybe you don't even need a salutation at all. "Good Morning" is nice. "Here's something new . . ." can get things off on the right foot. "Dear Fellow Bird Watcher" (or whatever) establishes context and relationship right away. There's no reason a salutation has to be a traditional one. Try all kinds of things . . . but first be sure that "Dear Friend" or "Dear Colleague" doesn't work, because if it is working, why change it? The fact that it bugs you doesn't matter. Does it affect response? That matters.

⹂

Dear Dr. Direct:

An order form in front of me right now says, "Please allow six to eight weeks for delivery." Isn't that too long to wait?

I won't order when I see that, and I see it all the time. I suspect it's either an attempt to circumvent the FTC's 30-day rule, or someone wants to make sure that all checks clear the bank before shipping.

Whichever it is, it's bad business. It's copy for the convenience of the advertiser. It's definitely not for the convenience of the customer. Most orders could go out the day they come in and no later than the next day. I buy obscure jazz CDs from a little company in New Jersey that promises "Credit card orders shipped the day they are received." Isn't that a great line? They offer the next best thing to instant gratification. Their shipping information actually gives me another reason to order now; those "six to eight weeks" people are giving me a reason not to order from them . . . ever.

∽

Dear Dr. Direct:

My boss is adamant. She says envelopes with no teasers are more effective because the people who get them won't know they contain advertising, so they'll tend to open them. Is this true?

Your boss may be right. Maybe. It depends on the kind of mailing you're doing. You probably don't have to put teasers on envelopes when you're writing to current customers. Your logo on the envelope will probably be enough to get it opened. What harm do teasers do, though?

And your boss might be on dangerous ground. If her intention is to trick prospects into thinking the mailing is not advertising, then how are they going to feel when they open the envelope and see it is advertising after all? Congratulations, you've fooled them. Now what? I've read that consumer mailings to cold lists are generally only about 70% as effective when there are no teasers on the outer envelope. I've always believed that an outer envelope's job is to get someone in the mood for what you have to say inside. There's one teaser I've always liked. Put the first line of a letter on the front of the outer envelope.

Good luck to all of you!

—Dr. Direct

PART

VIII

A Final Word

A FINAL WORD

Direct marketing works for all kinds of businesses. The idea is to make it work for yours, whether you have a service business or are selling a product.

1. **Plan to use direct marketing for the long haul.** That means write a plan, stick with it, and don't give up. Make testing a part of the plan, and test everything from offers to lists to creative approaches.

2. **Do the math for your program.** List all your costs for the product or service (including fulfillment) and the promotion, and make sure you are pricing correctly.

3. **Know your customers.** Send them surveys, ask them questions on the telephone. The more you understand them, the easier it will be to retain them. Remember that it costs a lot more to get a new customer than to keep the ones you already have.

4. **Be human.** In every communication with your prospects and customers, always let them see your personality. Talk about yourself, as it relates to what you're selling. This bonds you with customers and makes them like you, which is key in any selling situation.

5. **Include a guarantee with every offer.** People are buying from you on faith, so make sure they know they can return the product. It gives them the security they need to buy it in the first place.

6. **Prospect where your biggest potential is.** If you are a business looking for business clients, go to the best companies. Ask them for a small project, or a small order, so you can prove yourself. If you are selling a product go to lists of people who have bought similar products (in the mail).

7. **Hire professionals if you can afford it.** Copywriters and designers who work in direct marketing agencies often take on freelance assignments. Try to get the best people working on your program. That goes for media people as well. Tell them you want direct response rates (always less money) or remnant space.

A FINAL WORD (continued)

8. **Have a line of other products to offer your customers once they've purchased from you.** This business is about relationship marketing, so make sure your pipeline has new products to offer them all the time.

9. **Look for promotion partners.** You can work with other companies to offer products or services at special prices. For instance, if you are offering an exercise system, you might partner with a vitamin company to offer special discounts to your customers. Oil companies often partner with rental car companies, etc.

10. **Watch your mailbox.** See what the major mailers are doing and get ideas that way. If you receive the same kinds of offers as you are planning to offer, you know those offers are working. Read the trade publications, and learn as much as you can about direct marketing.

11. **Most of all, keep positive.** Don't get disappointed if your first or second or even third offer doesn't work as well as you hoped. Make it work. Try new offers, show your direct mail to friends, get input from family members, and be determined. Others, many others, have made fortunes in direct marketing, and so can you!

Write to us and tell us your success story. Maybe we'll include it in the next edition of this book!

Lois Geller
Mason & Geller, LLC
261 Madison Avenue
New York, NY 10016-2303
Phone: (212) 697-4477
Fax: (212) 697-2919
E-mail: lois_geller@masongeller.com

NOTES

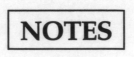

NOTES

NOTES